Praxis Core Math 5733 Study Guide
Updated Edition
with Mathematics Workbook
and Practice Tests
Academic Skills for Educators

Praxis Core Math 5733 Study Guide Updated Edition: with Mathematics Workbook and Practice Tests - Academic Skills for Educators

ISBN: 978-1-949282-73-3

For information on bulk discounts, please contact Exam SAM via our website.

Drawings in this publication are for guidance only. They are not drawn to scale.

NOTE: Praxis® and Praxis Core® are registered trademarks of Educational Testing Service (ETS). This publication is not associated with or endorsed by ETS.

Table of Contents

Praxis Core Math Test Format

The Praxis Core Mathematics Test 5733 contains the following types of questions:

- Number and Quantity – 20 questions
- Data Interpretation and Representation, Statistics, and Probability – 18 questions
- Algebra and Geometry – 18 questions

There are 56 questions in total on the Praxis Core math exam.

You will take the exam on a computer, unless you have applied for an exemption.

If you take the test on the computer, an on-screen calculator will be provided for you.

You will have 90 minutes to take the Praxis Core Math Test (5733).

Number and quantity questions cover the following skills:
- Positive and negative integers – including how to perform addition, subtraction, multiplication, and division, as well as understanding how to order numbers from highest to lowest or lowest to highest
- Mathematical equivalents and representing a value in more than one way – for example, converting a fraction to a decimal or percentage
- Whole numbers and their properties
- Ratios and proportion
- Decimals and percentages
- Dividing fractions by fractions
- Finding common factors and multiples
- US and metric systems of measurement

Data interpretation and representation, statistics, and probability questions cover:
- Reading and interpreting the visual display of quantitative information
- Understanding the relationship between data representation and data
- Making inferences form given visual displays of data
- Working with data and data representation to solve problems
- Analyzing scatterplots
- Interpreting distributions
- Drawing conclusions based on the data provided
- Calculating mean, median, mode, and range
- Calculating basic probability
- Using random sampling to draw conclusions about data
- Understanding probability models
- Understanding the difference between statistical and non-statistical questions

Algebra and geometry questions cover:
- Problem solving techniques for algebraic expressions, as well as real-life problems
- Equations and inequalities
- Solving expressions that contain one variable
- Finding equivalent expressions
- Narrative and mathematical representations of data
- Linear equations
- Simple quadratics
- Graphs
- Solving problems on geometric shapes
  - Triangles, rectangles, squares, and circles
  - Real-life problems on angles, area, perimeter, and box volume
  - Describing or drawing figures
  - Interpreting relationships between figures
- Pythagorean theorem
- Understanding congruency and similarity

Most of the questions will be multiple-choice, but there will be some numeric entry questions.

For the numeric entry questions, you have to make a calculation and provide the answer on your own. You will see a small box in which to place your answer, but you will not be provided with any answer choices.

You should also be aware that on some of the multiple-choice questions, you will be allowed to choose more than one response.

How to Use This Publication

Practice Test 1 of this study guide is in workbook format, with the questions organized by skill area and with study tips and solutions after each question.

The workbook format of practice test 1 will help you learn the strategies and formulas that you need to answer all of the types of questions on the actual Praxis Core Math Test.

You may wish to time yourself as you do the remaining practice tests in this book, allowing yourself 90 minutes for each exam. This will help to simulate the conditions of the actual test.

Praxis Core Math Practice Set 1 with Workbook

Number and Quantity Problems:

1) Which of the following shows the numbers ordered from least to greatest?

A) $-1/4$, $1/8$, $1/6$, 1
B) $-1/4$, $1/8$, 1 , $1/6$
C) $-1/4$, $1/6$, $1/8$, 1
D) $-1/4$, 1 , $1/8$, $1/6$
E) 1 , $1/6$, $1/8$, $-1/4$

greatest to least
1, $1/6$, $1/8$, $-1/4$

> In order to answer questions on ordering numbers from least to greatest or greatest to least, remember these principles: (a) Negative numbers are less than positive numbers; (b) When two fractions have the same numerator, the fraction with the smaller number in the denominator is the larger fraction.

The correct answer is A.

According to the principles above, $-1/4$ is less than $1/8$, $1/8$ is less than $1/6$, and $1/6$ is less than 1.

2) Consider the instructions in the chart below, and then answer the question that follows.

> Step 1: Begin with a number N.
>
> Step 2: Multiply the number by 3.
>
> Step 3: Subtract 4 from the result.
>
> Step 4: Divide the result by 8.

If the result of the calculation is 4, what is the value of N?
A) 1
B) 2
C) 12
D) 64
E) 0.667

> Work backwards, using inverse operations. So, if you are asked to divide you multiply to get the solution. If you are asked to subtract, you add to get the solution, and so on.

The correct answer is C.

Step 4 says "divide by 8," so multiply our final result of 4 by 8 to perform the first inverse operation: 4 × 8 = 32

Step 3 says "subtract 4," so add 4 to our previous result to perform the inverse operation: 32 + 4 = 36

Step 2 says "multiply by 3," so divide by 3 to perform the final inverse operation to solve: 36 ÷ 3 = 12

3) A recent report states that 72.8% of the work for the shopping center is now completed, and it has taken 182 days to do so. If work continues at the same rate, what fraction of the project will be completed after 43 more days? Put the correct amounts in the spaces provided.

First you need to divide the number of days into the percentage in order to determine what percentage of the project is being completed each day.

The correct answer is $^9/_{10}$.

As mentioned above, divide the percentage by the number of days in order to determine what percentage of the project is being completed each day:

72.8% ÷ 182 days = 0.4 percent completed per day

For the numerator of the fraction, we need to add 43 more days to the current 182 days: 182 + 43 = 225

Then determine how many days are needed to complete the entire project for the denominator of the fraction.

Since a complete project would be 100% complete, we divide the percentage per day into 100% to get the total days needed:

100% ÷ 0.4 = 250 days

Finally, express this as a simplified fraction:

$$\frac{225}{250} \div \frac{25}{25} = \frac{9}{10}$$

4) The temperature on Saturday was 62° F at 5:00 PM and 38° F at 11:00 PM. If the temperature fell at a constant rate on Saturday, what was the temperature at 9:00 PM?

A) 58° F
B) 54° F
C) 50° F
D) 46° F
E) 40° F

62 - 38 = 24
5pm to 11pm = 6 hours

This question assesses your knowledge of performing operations on integers. Here, we have to perform the operations of subtraction, multiplication, and division.

The correct answer is D.

First of all, you need to determine the difference in temperature during the entire time period: 62 – 38 = 24 degrees less

Then calculate how much time has passed. From 5:00 PM to 11:00 PM, 6 hours have passed.

Next, divide the temperature difference by the amount of time that has passed to get the temperature change per hour.

24 degrees ÷ 6 hours = 4 degrees less per hour

To calculate the temperature at the stated time, you need to calculate the time difference.

From 5:00 PM to 9:00 PM, 4 hours have passed. So, the temperature difference during the stated time is 4 hours × 4 degrees per hour = 16 degrees less.

Finally, deduct this from the beginning temperature to get your final answer.

62° F – 16° F = 46° F

5) A baker multiplied a recipe by $^1/_2$ when he should have divided the recipe by 4. Which one of the operations on the erroneous result will correct the error?

A) Divide by $^1/_2$

B) Multiply by $^1/_2$

C) Multiply by 2

D) Divide by 4

E) Multiply by 8

> For erroneous calculations that involve division, try to find an equivalent fraction for the division. The baker should have divided by 4. Dividing by 4 is equal to multiplying by what fraction?

The correct answer is B.

The baker should have divided the recipe by 4.

Dividing by four is the same as multiplying by $^1/_4$.

The baker erroneously multiplied by $^1/_2$, so he needs to multiply by $^1/_2$ again since $^1/_2 \times ^1/_2 = ^1/_4$.

6) A painter needs to paint 8 rooms, each of which have a surface area of 2000 square feet. If one bucket of paint covers 900 square feet, what is the fewest number of buckets of paint that must be used to complete all 8 rooms?

A) 3

B) 17

C) 18

D) 19

E) 20

> This is a question that requires you to find the fewest multiples of an item. Be mindful of the words "fewest" and "greatest" in problems like this one, since it will normally be impossible to purchase a fractional part of the item in the question. Therefore, you will need to round your result up or down accordingly.

The correct answer is C.

For your first step, determine how many square feet there are in total:
2000 square feet per room × 8 rooms = 16,000 square feet in total

$2000 \times 8 = 16,000$

Then you need to divide by the coverage rate:

16,000 square feet to cover ÷ 900 square feet coverage per bucket =
17.77 buckets needed

It is not possible to purchase a partial bucket of paint, so 17.77 is rounded up to
18 buckets of paint.

7) Soon Li jogged 3.6 miles in $^3/_4$ of an hour. What was her average jogging speed
in miles per hour?
A) 2.7
B) 4.0
C) 4.2
D) 4.6
E) 4.8

> This problem involves the calculation of miles per hour. To solve the
> problem, divide the distance traveled by the time in order to get the speed
> in miles per hour.

The correct answer is E.

As stated previously, divide the distance traveled by the time in order to get the
speed in miles per hour.

Remember that in order to divide by a fraction, you need to invert the fraction,
and then multiply.

3.6 miles ÷ $^3/_4$ = $3.6 \div {}^3/_4 = 3.6 \times {}^4/_3$

3.6 × $^4/_3$ = $(36 \times 4) \div 3 = 14.4 \div 3$

(3.6 × 4) ÷ 3 = $14.4 \div 3 = 4.8$

14.4 ÷ 3 = 4.8 miles per hour

8) When 1523.48 is divided by 100, which digit of the resulting number is in the tenths place?

A) 1
B) 2
C) 3
D) 4
E) 5

 *tenths, hundreds, thousandths,*

This question assesses your understanding of place value. Remember that the number after the decimal is in the tenths place, the second number after the decimal is in the hundredths place, and the third number after the decimal is in the thousandths place.

The correct answer is B.   *ten, ones, tenths, hundretts, thousandths, decimal   ten-thousanths*

Perform the division, and then check the decimal places of the numbers. Divide as follows: 1523.48 ÷ 100 = 15.2348

Reading our result from left to right: 1 is in the tens place, 5 is in the ones place, 2 is in the tenths place, 3 is in the hundredths place, 4 is in the thousandths place, and 8 is in the ten-thousandths place.

decimal

9) The price of a certain book is reduced from $60 to $45 at the end of the semester. By what percent is the price of the book reduced?

A) 15%
B) 20%
C) 25%
D) 33%
E) 45%

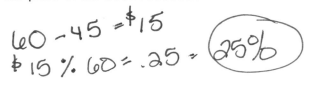 *60 − 45 = $15 $15 % 60 = .25 = 25%*

This question asks you to perform a calculation in order to determine the percentage discount on an item. Divide the dollar value of the reduction by the original price to get the percentage.

The correct answer is C.

Determine the dollar amount of the discount.

$60 original price – $45 sale price = $15 discount

Then divide the discount by the original price to get the percentage of the discount.

$15 ÷ $60 = 0.25 = 25%

10) Mr. Rodriguez teaches a class of 25 students. Ten of the students in his class participate in drama club. In which graph below does the dark gray area represent the percentage of students who participate in drama club?

A)

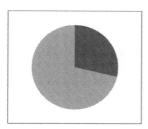

B)

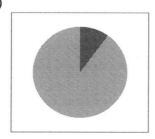

C)

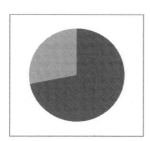

D)

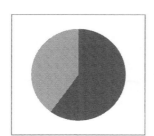

E)

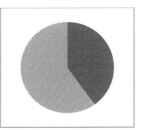

Questions like this one are asking you about how to express percentages graphically. Facts such as x students from y total students participate in a group can be represented as x/y.

The correct answer is E.

Ten out of 25 students participate in drama club.

First of all, express the relationship as a fraction: $10/25$

Then divide to find the percentage: $10/25 = 10 \div 25 = 0.40 = 40\%$

Finally, choose the pie chart that has 40% of its area shaded in dark gray.

40% is slightly less than half, so you need to choose chart E.

11) The ratio of males to females in the senior year class of Carson Heights High School was 6 to 7. If the total number of students in the class is 117, how many males are in the class?   6:7
   A) 48
   B) 54
   C) 56
   D) 58
   E) 63

Remember that a ratio can be expressed by using the word "to" or by separating the amounts in the subsets with a colon. So, our ratio is expressed as 6 to 7 or 6:7.

The correct answer is B.

For your first step, add the subsets of the ratio together: 6 + 7 = 13

Then divide this into the total: 117 ÷ 13 = 9

Finally, multiply the result from the previous step by the subset of males from the ratio: 6 × 9 = 54 males in the class

8

12) Results from a questionnaire administered to customers of a particular grocery store show that 4 out of 7 customers prefer toffee-flavored ice cream to coffee-flavored ice cream. Based on these results, if 1,540 customers purchased one of these two flavors of ice cream, how many of them would have purchased coffee-flavored ice cream?

A) 220
B) 420
C) 560
D) 660
E) 880

This is a question on a proportion, not on a ratio. Proportions often use the phrase "a out of b people." So, you need to do another step before you can get the ratio from the proportion.

The correct answer is D.

Be careful with the phrase "out of" in proportion questions like this one. We are given the phrase "4 out of 7."

7 - 4 = 3

If 4 out of 7 prefer the toffee flavor, then the remaining 3 prefer the coffee flavor.

Accordingly, the ratio of flavor preference of toffee to coffee is 4 to 3.

So, after determining the ratio, your next step is to divide the total by 7:

$1540 \div 7 = 220$

Then multiply this by 3 for the coffee-flavor preference: $220 \times 3 = 660$

13) A measurement of 116 feet is how many inches longer than a measurement of 36 yards?

A) 8
B) 80
C) 96
D) 960
E) 3,744

Convert yards to feet and then feet to inches. How many feet are in a yard? How many inches are in a foot? Refer to the appendix at the back of the book, if needed.

3 feet = 1 yard

The correct answer is C.

First of all, convert 36 yards to feet: 36 yards × 3 feet in a yard = 108 feet

Then subtract this from 116 feet: 116 − 108 = 8 feet

Then convert the feet to inches for your answer:

8 feet × 12 inches per foot = 96 inches

14) The graph below shows the relationship between the total number of hamburgers a restaurant sells and the total sales in dollars for the hamburgers. What is the sales price per hamburger?

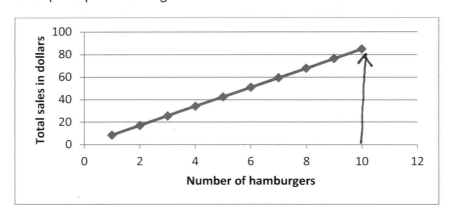

A) $4.00
B) $8.00
C) $8.50
D) $9.50
E) $10.00

Although the question involves a graph, it is essentially a number and quantity question involving division. To solve the problem, look at the graph and then divide the total sales in dollars for a particular number of units by the quantity sold in order to get the price per unit.

The correct answer is C.

For ten hamburgers, the total price is $85, so each hamburger sells for $8.50:
$85 total sales in dollars ÷ 10 hamburgers sold = $8.50 each

15) In Brown County Elementary School, parents are advised to have their children vaccinated against five childhood diseases. According to the chart below, how many children were vaccinated against at least three diseases?

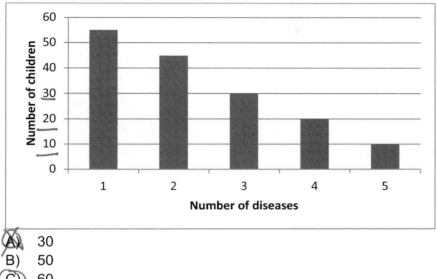

A) 30
B) 50
C) 60
D) 100
E) 130

For number and quantity questions that ask you to interpret bar graphs, you need to read the problem carefully to determine what is represented on the horizontal axis (bottom) and the vertical axis (left side) of the graph.

The correct answer is C.

The quantity of diseases is indicated on the bottom of the graph, while the number of children is indicated on the left side of the graph.

To determine the number of children that have been vaccinated against three or more diseases, we need to add the amounts represented by the bars for 3, 4, and 5 diseases: 30 + 20 + 10 = 60 children

16) In a sequence of integers, the first number is N and each number in the sequence thereafter is half of the previous number. If the sixth integer in the sequence is 4, what is the first integer?
A) 256
B) 192
C) 128
D) 108
E) 64

When you are given the final term in a sequence and asked for a previous term, you need to divide by the size of the increment to solve. Here, our increment is one-half.

The correct answer is C.

Remember to divide by the size of the increment to solve. Again, our increment is one-half.

When we divide by one-half, we need to multiply by two since $1 \div \frac{1}{2} = 2$.

So, multiply like this to solve:

Term 6: 4; Term 5: $4 \times 2 = 8$; Term 4: $8 \times 2 = 16$; Term 3: $16 \times 2 = 32$; Term 2: $32 \times 2 = 64$; Term 1: $64 \times 2 = 128$

17) What is the greatest common divisor of the following integers? 204 and 272
A) 72
B) 68
C) 34
D) 24
E) 4

The greatest common divisor is the largest number that will divide into at least two other numbers.

The correct answer is B.

Here our greatest common divisor is 68 since $204 \div 68 = 3$ and $272 \div 68 = 4$.

If you feel stuck, divide by the first obvious number you can think of, and keep dividing until you can't do any further division.

For example, first you could divide by 4:

204 ÷ 4 = 51 and 272 ÷ 4 = 68

Then see if you can divide further. Be sure to consider the prime numbers as possible divisors.

Both 51 and 68 from above are divisible by 17, so divide as shown:

51 ÷ 17 = 3 and 68 ÷ 17 = 4

Then multiply the individual divisors together to get the greatest common divisor:

4 × 17 = 68

18) Susan is trying to limit her caffeine intake. She has a coffee in the morning every third day and a glass of iced tea every fourth day in the afternoon. For how many of the next 90 days will Susan consume coffee and iced tea on the same day?

A) 7
B) 10
C) 12
D) 22
E) 30

> For interval questions like this one, multiply the number of days of each interval together to get the day on which the intervals will coincide.

The correct answer is A.

Every twelfth day, Susan will have both drinks on the same day.

We get this result by multiplying 3 days for the coffee interval by 4 days for the tea interval: 3 × 4 = 12

Then we have to determine how many 12-day intervals there are in 90 days. We do this by dividing 90 by 12: 90 ÷ 12 = 7.5

We don't count the half day, so the answer is 7.

19) Which of the equations provided below is sufficient to illustrate that the following statement is false?

| If x × y can be divided by 6, then x is divisible by 6 or y is divisible by 6. |

A) $4 \times 5 = 20$
B) $3 \times 4 = 12$
C) $6 \times 3 = 18$
D) $5 \times 6 = 30$
E) $8 \times 6 = 48$

This question is asking you to find counter-examples to a statement by using basic operations. First of all, rule out all answer choices that include a factor that is the same as the divisor stated in the facts of the question.

The correct answer is B.

Answers C, D, and E all multiply another number by 6. These factors of 6 are of course divisible by 6, which supports the statement above instead of disproving it.

Answer A is irrelevant since neither the factors nor the product is divisible by 6.

Answer B disproves the statement because 12 is divisible by 6, although neither 3 nor 4 is divisible by 6.

20) In a particular section of a library, the ratio of non-fiction books to fiction books is 7 to 9. The total number of fiction and non-fiction books in this section of the library is 128. If 10 fiction books and 14 non-fiction books are retired and removed from this section of the library, what fraction of the remaining books in this section are fiction? Put the correct amounts in the spaces provided.

$$\frac{\boxed{}}{\boxed{}}$$

This is an advanced question on ratios. First, add the two parts of the ratio together. Then divide this result into the total number of books. Then multiply each part of the ratio by this result to get the number of each type of book.

The correct answer is 31 / 52.

Add the two parts of the ratio together: 7 + 9 = 16

Then divide this into the total number of books: 128 ÷ 16 = 8

Then multiply each part of the ratio by 8 to get the number of each type of book:

7 × 8 = 56 non-fiction books

9 × 8 = 72 fiction books

Then subtract the removals and find the new total:

56 − 14 = 42 non-fiction left

72 − 10 = 62 fiction left

42 + 62 = 104 total books left

Finally, express the fiction books as a fraction of the total: 62 / 104 = 31 / 52

Data Interpretation and Representation:

21)   A mother has noticed that the more sugar her child eats, the more her child
       sleeps at night. Which of the following graphs best illustrates the relationship
       between the amount of sugar the child consumes and the child's amount of
       sleep?

A)

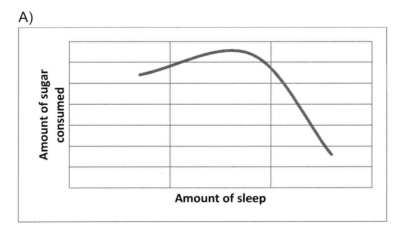

B)

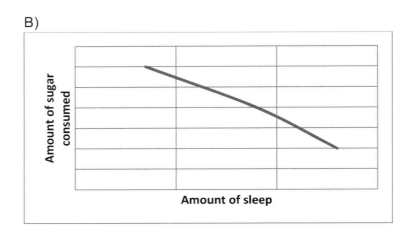

C)

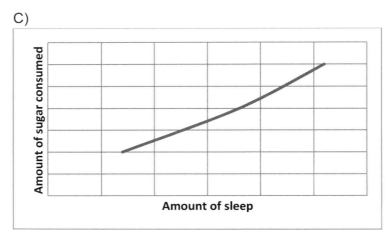

D)

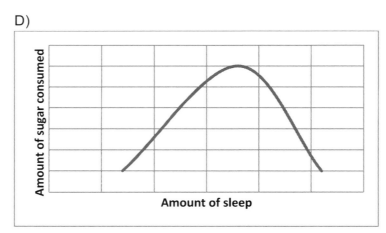

E)

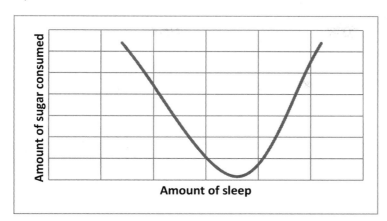

Your exam will have problems like this one that show graphs or scatterplots that represent the relationship between two variables. Be sure that you know the difference between positive linear relationships and negative linear relationships for the exam. In a positive linear relationship, an increase in one variable is correlated to an increase in the other variable, meaning that the line will point upwards from left to right.

In a negative linear relationship, an increase in one variable is correlated to a decrease in the other variable, meaning that the line will point downwards from left to right.

The correct answer is C.

As the quantity of sugar increases, the amount of sleep also increases.

A positive linear relationship therefore exists between the two variables. This is represented in chart C since the amount of sleep is greater when the amount of sugar consumed is higher.

22) Which one of the scatterplots below most strongly suggests a negative linear relationship between x and y?

A)

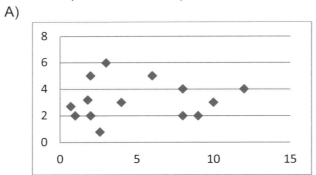

B)

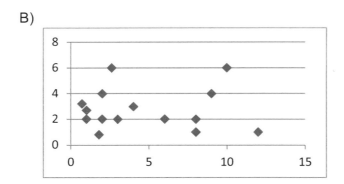

C)

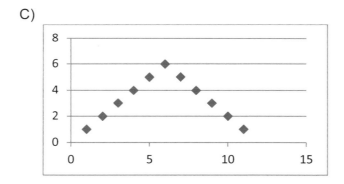

D)

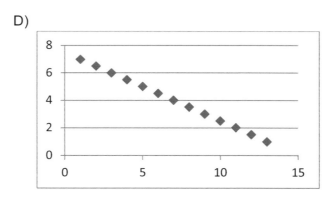

E)

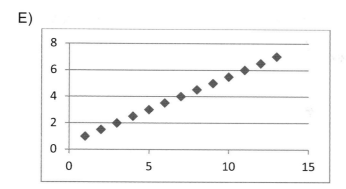

Your exam will have problems containing scatterplots like those above. For these types of questions, you will need to look at each scatterplot and determine which one has the dots in a configuration most similar to the one in the question. As stated in the previous problem, be sure that you know the difference between positive linear relationships and negative linear relationships for the exam.

The correct answer is D.

A negative linear relationship exists when an increase in one variable results in a decrease in the other variable. This is represented by chart D.

Go on to the next page.

23) The scatterplot provided below shows the relationship between the average hours of exercise each person had per day (H) and their strength ratings (S) on a scale of 1 to 5. Which of the following statements best describes the relationship between H and S?

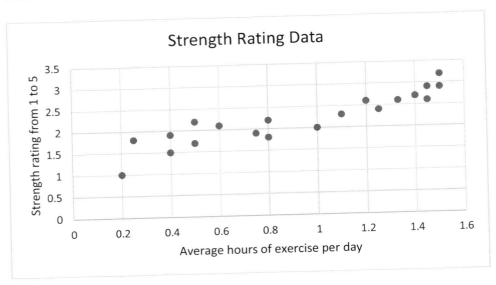

A) Increased amounts of exercise cause increases in performance ratings.
B) High strength ratings lead to increased amounts of exercise.
C) There is a positive linear relationship between H and S.
D) There is a negative linear relationship between H and S.
E) No relationship can be observed from the data.

This is a question on correlation on causation. For these types of questions, remember that correlation and causation are not the same. In other words, we cannot conclusively say that one variable causes another variable to happen when looking at data. We can only say that there is a correlation between the variables.

The correct answer is C.

From the chart, we can see that as the amount of exercise increases, the strength rating also increases. As mentioned previously, this is known as a positive linear relationship.

Be careful about answers A and B. They both are implying that there is a cause-and-effect relationship, rather than correctly identifying a correlation.

24) The pictograph below shows the number of pizzas sold in one day at a local pizzeria. Cheese pizzas sold for $10 each, pepperoni pizzas sold for $12, and the total sales of all three types of pizza was $310. What is the sales price of one vegetable pizza?

Cheese	▼ ▼ ▼
Pepperoni	▼ ▼
Vegetable	▼

Each ▼ represents 5 pizzas.

A) $5
B) $8
C) $9
D) $10
E) $12

This is an example of an exam question on interpreting data from pictographs. Each symbol on the pictograph represents a certain quantity of items, so remember to multiply by that amount in order to determine the totals for each group.

The correct answer is B.

First, determine how many cheese and pepperoni pizzas were sold. Each triangle symbol represents 5 pizzas.

Therefore, 15 cheese pizzas were sold:

3 symbols on the pictograph × 5 pizzas per symbol = 15 cheese pizzas

We also know that 10 pepperoni pizzas were sold:

2 symbols on the pictograph × 5 pizzas per symbol = 10 pepperoni pizzas

Then determine the value of these two types of pizzas based on the prices stated in the problem:

(15 cheese pizzas × $10 each) + (10 pepperoni pizzas × $12 each) =

$150 + $120 = $270

The remaining amount is allocable to the vegetable pizzas:

Total sales of $310 – $270 = $40 worth of vegetable pizzas

Since each triangle represents 5 pizzas, 5 vegetable pizzas were sold. We calculate the price of the vegetable pizzas as follows:

$40 worth of vegetable pizzas ÷ 5 vegetable pizzas sold = $8 per vegetable pizza

25) A zoo has reptiles, birds, quadrupeds, and fish. At the start of the year, they have a total of 1,500 creatures living in the zoo. The pie chart below shows percentages by category for the 1,500 creatures at the start of the year.

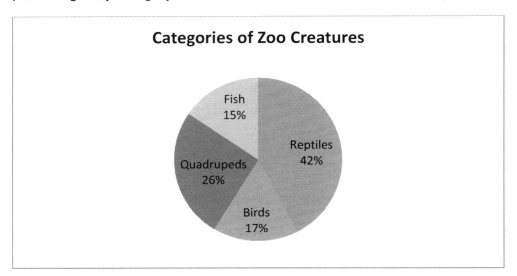

Categories of Zoo Creatures

Fish 15%
Reptiles 42%
Quadrupeds 26%
Birds 17%

At the end of the year, the zoo still has 1,500 creatures, but reptiles constitute 40%, birds 23%, and quadrupeds 21%. How many more fish were there at the end of the year than at the beginning of the year?
A) 10
B) 11
C) 15
D) 16
E) 150

This question is asking you to interpret a pie chart that shows percentages by category. If you are asked to calculate changes to the data in the categories in the chart, be sure to multiply by the percentages at the beginning of the year and then do a separate calculation using the percentages at the end of the year.

The correct answer is C.

At the beginning of the year, 15% of the 1,500 creatures were fish, so there were 225 fish at the beginning of the year: 1,500 × 0.15 = 225

In order to find the percentage of fish at the end of the year, we first need to add up the percentages for the other animals: 40% + 23% + 21% = 84%

Then subtract this amount from 100% to get the remaining percentage for the fish: 100% − 84% = 16%

Multiply the percentage by the total to get the number of fish at the end of the year: 1,500 × 0.16 = 240

Then subtract the beginning of the year from the end of the year to calculate the increase in the number of fish: 240 − 225 = 15

Go on to the next page.

26) The scatterplot below shows the relationship between the average number of visits to the recycling center per family per week for a given year and the amounts of garbage generated daily for these 25 families for the same year. For those families generating more than 1.5 pounds of garbage per day, what fraction had more than 2 trips to the recycling center per week?

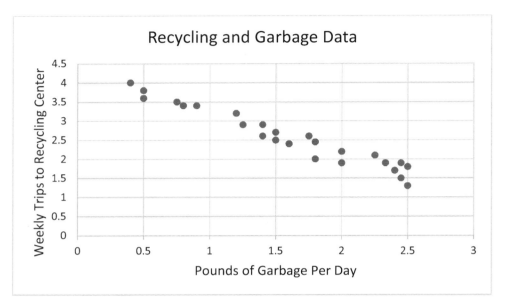

A) $\frac{1}{3}$

B) $\frac{1}{5}$

C) $\frac{6}{25}$

D) $\frac{7}{25}$

E) $\frac{8}{25}$

Read the facts carefully and then analyze the scatterplot. We need garbage amounts greater than 1.5 and recycling amounts more than 2. Be sure not to include the dots that are exactly 1.5 or 2, respectively, as the question is asking for amounts over these two figures.

The correct answer is B.

There are five dots on the scatterplot that have garbage amounts greater than 1.5 and recycling amounts more than 2, as indicated in the rectangle in the scatterplot below.

So, 5 out of 25 families meet the criteria for a fraction of $^5/_{25}$ or $^1/_5$.

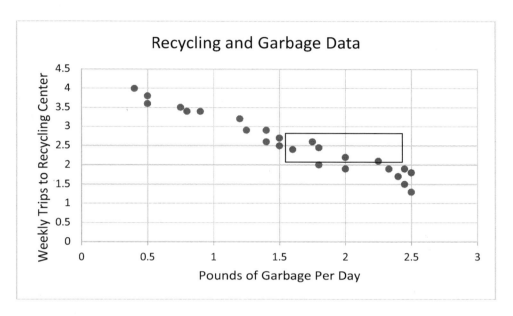

27) Use the information below to answer the question that follows.

- Classes in the morning last for 45 minutes, but classes in the afternoon last for 50 minutes.
- Lunch begins promptly at 12:30 pm and finishes promptly at 1:00 pm.
- There are 3 classes after lunch and 4 classes before lunch.
- There are no breaks between classes or between classes and lunch.

Which one of the following statements could be true?
A) Classes begin at 9:30 am.
B) Classes begin at 10:00 m.
C) The second class after lunch begins at 2:00 pm.
D) The second class after lunch begins at 2:50 pm.
E) The last class of the day ends at 3:10 pm.

To answer these types of questions, read each of the answer choices one by one. Then compare each answer to the information provided to determine if that answer is true or false.

The correct answer is A.

If classes last for 45 minutes and there are 4 classes before lunch, the morning classes last for 3 hours in total:

45 minutes × 4 = 180 minutes = 3 hours

If lunch begins at 12:30, it is therefore possible for classes to begin three hours earlier at 9:30.

28) Which of the following methods of data representation would be best to represent the population of a certain city for each of the past ten years?
A) scatterplot
B) pie chart
C) bar graph
D) 3-D illustration
E) storyboard

For questions on data representation, remember the following:
A scatterplot is used to see what kind of relationship exists between two items or events.
A pie chart is useful to represent the amount or percentage of each group to the total of all groups.
Bar graphs and line charts are usually used to represent changes to amounts over time.
3-D illustrations are useful for giving instructions on how to assemble something.
Storyboards are visual representations used by graphic artists. They are not used for data.

The correct answer is C.

In the bar graph, you will have bars for all of the years, with each bar representing the amount of the population that year.

This would make it easy to see the changes to the population over time. A line graph would also be suitable, although that is not a choice for this question.

Statistics and Probability Problems:

29) The ages of 5 siblings are: 2, 5, 7, 12, and x. If the mean age of the 5 siblings is 8 years old, what is the age (x) of the 5th sibling?
A) 8
B) 10
C) 12
D) 14
E) 16

> This is a problem on determining the value that is missing from the calculation of a mean of a set of values. Remember that the mean is the same thing as the arithmetic average. In order to calculate the mean, you simply add up the values of all of the items in the set, and then divide by the number of items in the set. To solve problems like this one, set up an equation to calculate the mean, using x for the unknown value.

The correct answer is D.

Set up your equation to calculate the average, using x for the age of the 5th sibling:

$(2 + 5 + 7 + 12 + x) \div 5 = 8$

$(2 + 5 + 7 + 12 + x) \div 5 \times 5 = 8 \times 5$

$(2 + 5 + 7 + 12 + x) = 40$

$26 + x = 40$

$26 - 26 + x = 40 - 26$

$x = 14$

30) Members of a weight loss group report their individual weight loss to the group leader every week. During the week, the following amounts in pounds were reported: 1, 1, 3, 2, 4, 3, 1, 2, and 1.
What is the mode of the weight loss for the group?
A) 1 pound
B) 2 pounds
C) 3 pounds
D) 4 pounds
E) 18 pounds

This is a question on mode. Mode is the value that occurs most frequently in a data set. For example, if 10 students scored 85 on a test, 6 students scored 90, and 4 students scored 80, the mode score is 85.

The correct answer is A.

The mode is the number that occurs the most frequently in the set.

Our data set is: 1, 1, 3, 2, 4, 3, 1, 2, 1.

The number 1 occurs 4 times in the set, which is more frequently than any other number in the set, so the mode is 1.

31) Mark's record of times for the 400-meter freestyle at swim meets this season is:

8.19, 7.59, 8.25, 7.35, 9.10

What is the median of his times?

A) 7.59
B) 8.19
C) 8.25
D) 8.096
E) 40.48

This question is asking you to find the median of a set of numbers. The median is the number that is in the middle of the set when the numbers are in ascending order.

The correct answer is B.

The problem provides the number set: 8.19, 7.59, 8.25, 7.35, 9.10

First of all, put the numbers in ascending order: 7.35, 7.59, 8.19, 8.25, 9.10

Then find the one that is in the middle: 7.35, 7.59, **8.19**, 8.25, 9.10

32) A student receives the following scores on her assignments during the term:

98.5, 85.5, 80.0, 97, 93, 92.5, 93, 87, 88, 82

What is the range of her scores?

A) 17.0
B) 18.0
C) 18.5
D) 89.65
E) 93.0

> This is a question on calculating range. To calculate range, the lowest value in the data set is deducted from the highest value in the data set.

The correct answer is C.

To calculate the range, the low number in the set is deducted from the high number in the set.

The problem set is: 98.5, 85.5, 80.0, 97, 93, 92.5, 93, 87, 88, 82.

The high number is 98.5 and the low number is 80, so the range is 18.5 since $98.5 - 80 = 18.5$

33) An owner of a carnival attraction draws teddy bears out of a bag at random to give to prize winners. She has 10 brown teddy bears, 8 white teddy bears, 4 black teddy bears, and 2 pink teddy bears when she opens the attraction at the start of the day. The first prize winner of the day receives a brown teddy bear. What is the probability that the second prize winner will receive a pink teddy bear?

A) $1/24$

B) $1/23$

C) $2/24$

D) $2/23$

E) $1/2$

This is a question on calculating basic probability. First of all, calculate how many items there are in total in the data set, which is also called the "sample space" or (S). Then reduce the data set if further items are removed. Probability can be expressed as a fraction. The number of items available in the total data set at the time of the draw goes in the denominator. The chance of the desired outcome, which is also referred to as the event or (E), goes in the numerator of the fraction. You can determine the chance of the event by calculating how many items are available in the subset of the desired outcome.

The correct answer is D.

You need to determine the number of possible outcomes at the start of the day first of all.

The owner has 10 brown teddy bears, 8 white teddy bears, 4 black teddy bears, and 2 pink teddy bears when she opens the attraction at the start of the day. So, at the start of the day, she has 24 teddy bears: $10 + 8 + 4 + 2 = 24$

Then you need to reduce this amount by the quantity of items that have been removed. The problem tells us that she has given out a brown teddy bear, so there are 23 teddy bears left in the sample space: $24 - 1 = 23$

The event is the chance of the selection of a pink teddy bear. We know that there are two pink teddy bears left after the first prize winner receives their prize.

Finally, we need to put the event (the number representing the chance of the desired outcome) in the numerator and the number of possible remaining combinations (the sample space) in the denominator.

So, the answer is $^2/_{23}$.

34) A magician pulls colored scarves out of a hat at random. The hat contains 5 red scarves and 6 blue scarves. The other scarves in the hat are green. If a scarf is pulled out of the hat at random, the probability that the scarf is red is $^1/_3$. How many green scarves are in the hat?
A) 3
B) 4
C) 5
D) 6
E) 7

This question is asking you to determine the value missing from a sample space when calculating basic probability. This is like other problems on basic probability, but we need to work backwards to find the missing value. First, set up an equation to find the total items in the sample space. Then subtract the quantities of the known subsets from the total in order to determine the missing value.

The correct answer is B.

First, we will use variable T as the total number of items in the set. The probability of getting a red scarf is $^1/_3$.

So, set up an equation to find the total items in the data set.

$$\frac{5}{T} = \frac{1}{3}$$

$$\frac{5}{T} \times 3 = \frac{1}{3} \times 3$$

$$\frac{5}{T} \times 3 = 1$$

$$\frac{15}{T} = 1$$

$$\frac{15}{T} \times T = 1 \times T$$

$$15 = T$$

We have 5 red scarves, 6 blue scarves, and x green scarves in the data set that make up the total sample space, so now subtract the amount of red and blue scarves from the total in order to determine the number of green scarves.

$$5 + 6 + x = 15$$

$$11 + x = 15$$

$$11 - 11 + x = 15 - 11$$

$$x = 4$$

35) Becky rolls a fair pair of six-sided dice. One of the die is black and the other is red. Each die has values from 1 to 6. What is the probability that Becky will roll a 4 on the red die and a 5 on the black die?

A) $^1/_{36}$

B) $^2/_{36}$

C) $^1/_{12}$

D) $^2/_{12}$

E) $^{10}/_{12}$

This is an advanced problem on understanding probability models. For these questions, you will usually have two items, like two dice or a coin and a die. Each item will have various outcomes, like heads or tails for the coin or the different numbers on the die. To solve problems like this one, it is usually best to write out the possible outcomes in a list. This will help you visualize the number of possible outcomes that make up the sample space. Then circle or highlight the events from the list to get your answer.

The correct answer is A.

In this case, we have two items, each of which has a variable outcome. There are 6 numbers on the black die and 6 numbers on the red die.

Using multiplication, we can see that there are 36 possible combinations: 6 × 6 = 36

To check your answer, you can list the possibilities of the various combinations:

(1,1) (1,2) (1,3) (1,4) (1,5) (1,6)
(2,1) (2,2) (2,3) (2,4) (2,5) (2,6)
(3,1) (3,2) (3,3) (3,4) (3,5) (3,6)
(4,1) (4,2) (4,3) (4,4) (4,5) (4,6)
(5,1) (5,2) (5,3) **(5,4)** (5,5) (5,6)
(6,1) (6,2) (6,3) (6,4) (6,5) (6,6)

If the number on the left in each set of parentheses represents the black die and the number on the right represents the red die, we can see that there is one chance that Becky will roll a 4 on the red die and a 5 on the black die.

The result is expressed as a fraction, with the event (chance of the desired outcome) in the numerator and the total sample space (total data set) in the denominator.

So, the answer is $^1/_{36}$.

36) The school board wants to poll a sample of students to get their opinions on dropping the music program in favor of having more sports programs. Which one of the following methods will result in the most statistically valid information about the opinions of all of the students at the high school?
A) To select ten students at random from each grade at the school
B) To speak to all of the members of the high school football team
C) To ask two members of each grade at random as they leave band practice
D) To give questionnaires out to the freshmen and sophomore students
E) To gather the opinions from students who are willing to speak to the school board

This question is asking you about how best to use random sampling to draw conclusions about data. For information to be statistically valid, the data must be taken at random from a sample set of respondents that best represents the entire group.

The correct answer is A.

Our entire group in this problem is all of the students at the high school. So, it would be best to select ten students at random from each grade at the school.

The other answer choices would be biased in favor of members of certain groups, namely football players (answer B), band participants (answer C), younger students (answer D), and students who are not afraid to speak to the school board (answer E).

37) Which of the following are statistical questions? You may select more than one answer.

_____ (1) How long is that piece of string?

_____ (2) How many customers go to that coffee shop on Saturdays?

_____ (3) What time is history class?

_____ (4) How do students rate Mrs. Brown's calculus class?

_____ (5) What are the perimeter measurements of the high school parking lot?

Statistical questions usually ask about opinions and behaviors. In addition, statistical questions can have a variety of different answers. On the other hand, questions about measuring time and distance are non-statistical questions because they have only one possible answer.

The correct answers are (2) and (4).

"How many customers go to that coffee shop on Saturdays?" is a statistical question because the number of customers in the shop can be counted. The number will also vary every Saturday.

"How do students rate Mrs. Brown's calculus class?" is also a statistical question because some students will have positive opinions, others will have negative opinions, and still others will have mixed opinions. In addition, the various ratings can be counted.

Algebra Problems:

38) If $\frac{3}{4}x - 2 = 4$, $x =$?

A) $\frac{8}{3}$

B) $\frac{1}{8}$

C) 8

D) –8

E) 24

This is a problem requiring you to solve an expression that contains a single variable, a fraction, and integers. First, isolate the integers and then eliminate the fraction. Finally, divide to find the value of the variable.

The correct answer is C.

Isolate the integers to one side of the equation.

$$\frac{3}{4}x - 2 = 4$$

$$\frac{3}{4}x - 2 + 2 = 4 + 2$$

$$\frac{3}{4}x = 6$$

Then get rid of the fraction by multiplying both sides by the denominator.

$$\frac{3}{4}x \times 4 = 6 \times 4$$

$$3x = 24$$

Then divide to solve the problem.

$$3x \div 3 = 24 \div 3$$

$$x = 8$$

39) If $2(3x - 1) = 4(x + 1) - 3$, what is the value of x? State your answer as a fraction in the spaces provided.

Numerator value of x = _____

Denominator value of x = _____

This problem requires you to solve an algebraic expression that contains one variable (x) on both sides of the equation. When the variable is used on both sides of the equation, you should perform the multiplication on the parentheticals first. Then isolate x to solve the problem.

The correct answers are 3 (numerator value) and 2 (denominator value).

Perform the multiplication on the terms in the parentheses.
$2(3x - 1) = 4(x + 1) - 3$
$6x - 2 = (4x + 4) - 3$

Then simplify.
$6x - 2 = 4x + 4 - 3$
$6x - 2 = 4x + 1$
$6x - 2 - 1 = 4x + 1 - 1$
$6x - 3 = 4x$

Then isolate x to get your answer.

$6x - 3 = 4x$

$6x - 4x - 3 = 4x - 4x$

$2x - 3 = 0$

$2x - 3 + 3 = 0 + 3$

$2x = 3$

$2x \div 2 = 3 \div 2$

$x = {}^3\!/_2$

40) In a group of 150 athletes, 75 are marathon runners, as represented by circle M, and 45 are triathletes, as represented by circle T. If 25 athletes are both marathon runners and triathletes, how many of the athletes are neither marathon runners nor triathletes?

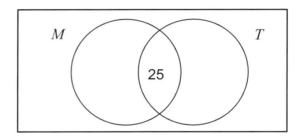

A) 30
B) 45
C) 55
D) 70
E) 95

> In a Venn diagram, the number of items in the intersection where the circles overlap is included in both groups. Be sure not to double count these items.

The correct answer is C.

First, add the number of marathon runners and triathletes together: 75 + 45 = 120

Then subtract 25 from this amount as it would have been double-counted since these athletes were in both groups: 120 – 25 = 95

Then subtract this from the total to determine how many other athletes there are: 150 – 95 = 55

41) Which of the following equations is equivalent to $\frac{x}{5} + \frac{y}{2}$?

A) $\frac{x + y}{7}$

B) $\frac{2x + 5y}{10}$

C) $\frac{5x + 2y}{10}$

D) $\frac{2x + 5y}{7}$

E) $\frac{5y}{2x}$

This problem is asking you to find an equivalent expression for a mathematical equation that contains fractions. To add fractions, find the lowest common denominator first and then add the numerators.

The correct answer is B.

You need to find the lowest common denominator. Then add the numerators together as shown.

$$\frac{x}{5} + \frac{y}{2} =$$

$$\left(\frac{x}{5} \times \frac{2}{2}\right) + \left(\frac{y}{2} \times \frac{5}{5}\right) =$$

$$\frac{2x}{10} + \frac{5y}{10} =$$

$$\frac{2x + 5y}{10}$$

42) Which of the following steps will solve the equation for x: $4x - 3 = 2$
A) Add 3 to both sides of the equation, and then divide both sides by 4.
B) Add 3 to both sides of the equation, and then subtract 4 from both sides.
C) Add 2 to both sides of the equation, and then divide both sides by 4.
D) Subtract 2 from both sides of the equation, and then divide both sides by −3.
E) Divide both sides of the equations by 4, and then subtract 3 from both sides.

For this question, you need to find the answer that provides a narrative explanation for the solution to the problem, rather than calculating the solution itself.

The correct answer is A.

Remember that to solve problems like this, you need to deal with the integers (whole numbers) and then isolate the variable (x).

The solution is as follows:

$4x - 3 = 2$

$4x - 3 + 3 = 2 + 3$ (Add 3 to both sides of the equation.)

$4x = 5$

$4x \div 4 = 5 \div 4$ (Divide both sides by 4.)

$x = \frac{5}{4}$

43) Toby is going to buy a car. The total purchase price of the car is represented by variable C. He will pay D dollars immediately, and then he will make equal payments (P) each month for a certain number of months (M). Which equation below represents the amount of his monthly payment (P)?

A) $\frac{C-D}{M}$

B) $\frac{C}{M} - D$

C) $\frac{M}{C-D}$

D) $D - \frac{C}{M}$

E) $\frac{C}{M}$

This problem requires you to set up an algebraic equation based on facts in a real-life problem. In this problem, we need to calculate a monthly payment after a down payment has been made. Deduct the down payment from the purchase price, and then divide by the number of months to solve the problem.

The correct answer is A.

The total amount that Toby has to pay is represented by C.

He is paying D dollars immediately, so we can determine the remaining amount that he owes by deducting his down payment from the total.

So, the remaining amount owing is represented by the equation: C − D

We have to divide the remaining amount owing by the number of months (M) to get the monthly payment (P):

$$P = (C - D) \div M = \frac{C-D}{M}$$

44) Fatima drove into town at a rate of 50 miles per hour. She shopped in town for 20 minutes, and then drove home on the same route at a rate of 60 miles per hour. Which of the following equations best expresses the total time (Tt) that it took Fatima to make the journey and do the shopping? Note that the variable D represents the distance in miles from Fatima's house to town.

A) $Tt + 20 \text{ minutes} = 110 \times D$

B) $Tt + 20 \text{ minutes} = [(50 + 60) \div 2] \times D$

C) $Tt = [(D \div 50) + (D \div 60)] + 20 \text{ minutes}$

D) $Tt = D \div 110$

E) $Tt = (D \div 110) + 20 \text{ minutes}$

> This problem asks you to set up an algebraic equation based on facts in a real-life problem. In this problem, we need to calculate the time spent on a journey. Read the problem carefully and make sure that all of the required facts are represented in your final equation.

The correct answer is C.

The amount of time in hours (T) multiplied by miles per hour (mph) gives us the distance traveled (D).

So, the equation for distance traveled is: $T \times \text{mph} = D$

The problem tells us that we need to calculate T, so we need to isolate T by changing our equation as follows:

$T \times \text{mph} = D$

$(T \times \text{mph}) \div \text{mph} = D \div \text{mph}$

$T = D \div \text{mph}$

In our problem, Fatima drives home on the same route that she took into town, so we need to calculate the traveling time for the journey into town, as well as for the journey home:

$(D \div 50) + (D \div 60) = T$

Then add back the 20 minutes she spent in town to get the total time:

$Tt = [(D \div 50) + (D \div 60)] + 20 \text{ minutes}$

45) A baseball team sells T-shirts and sweatpants to the public for a fundraising event. The total amount of money the team earned from these sales was $850. Variable t represents the number of T-shirts sold and variable s represents the number of sweatpants sold. The total sales in dollars is represented by the equation $25t + 30s$. The amount earned by selling sweatpants is what fraction of the total amount earned?

A) $s/850$
B) $30s/850$
C) $(25t + 30s)/850$
D) $t/850$
E) $25t/850$

> This problem asks you to express part of an algebraic equation as a fraction of the entire equation. You can sometimes substitute a numerical or dollar value in the expression, as in this problem.

The correct answer is B.

We need to set up a fraction, the numerator of which consists of the amount of sales in dollars for sweatpants, and the denominator of which consists of the total amount of sales in dollars for both items.

The problem tells us that the amount of sales in dollars for sweatpants is $30s$ and the total amount of sales is $850, so the answer is $30s/850$.

46) The information provided in the box below describes three locations on a map. Use the information provided to answer the question that follows.

> • The police station is 10 miles away from the fire station
> • The fire station is 6 miles away from the hospital.

Based on the information in the box, what conclusions can be made?
A) The police station is no more than 6 miles away from the hospital.
B) The police station is no more than 10 miles away from the hospital.
C) The police station is exactly 6 miles away from the hospital.
D) The police station is no more than 16 miles away from the hospital.
E) No conclusions may be made since essential information is missing.

> Read the facts carefully for questions involving maps and then make conclusions based on the information provided. You may find it helpful to draw diagrams to help you answer these types of questions. For some questions, a diagram may be provided.

The correct answer is D.

For questions about distance like this one, keep in mind that the locations may or may not lie on a straight line. For example, the locations could be laid out on the map like this:

Police station   Fire station   Hospital

10 miles   6 miles

In the layout above, the police station would be 16 miles from the hospital.

However, the locations could also be laid out like this:

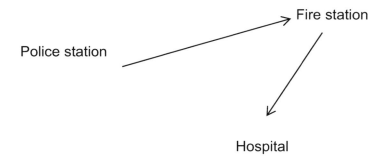

Fire station

Police station

Hospital

We can see that the locations will be the farthest from each other if they are laid out on a straight line as in the first example above.

In other words, a person could always go to the hospital by traveling to the fire station from the police station (10 miles) and then traveling from the fire station to the hospital (6 miles).

Therefore, the police station would never be more than 16 miles away from the hospital, regardless of the layout.

47) The following three locations are on a map of an amusement park: Ferris wheel, roller coaster, and entrance. On the map, which is drawn to scale, the distance between the Ferris wheel and the entrance is 8 inches, and the distance between the entrance and the roller coaster is 6.5 inches. The actual distance between the Ferris wheel and the entrance is 350 yards. What is the actual distance between the entrance and the roller coaster to the nearest yard?
A) 294
B) 284
C) 350
D) 360
E) 43.75

For questions about scale, divide the actual distance by the corresponding distance on the map to get the scale of the map.

The correct answer is B.

The actual distance between the Ferris wheel and the entrance is 350 yards, and this is represented by 8 inches on the map, so divide to get the scale:

$350 \div 8 = 43.75$

In other words, every inch on the map represents 43.75 yards.

Now multiply the scale of the map by the number of inches between the entrance and the roller coaster to get the actual distance: $6.5 \times 43.75 = 284.375$

Finally, round to 284 yards.

48) Indicate which of the following statements are true for all positive numbers x, y and z. You may choose more than one answer.
A) $x \times (y + z) = (y + z) \times x$
B) $x - (y + z) = x - y + z$
C) $x \times (y + z) = (x \times y) + z$
D) $x + (y - z) = (x + y) - z$

The correct answers are A and D.

Answer A is true because of the communicative property of multiplication. In other words, $x \times y = y \times x$

Answer D is true because y is a positive number and z, as a negative number, is the last operation to be performed on both sides of the equation.

Geometry Problems:

49) The figure shown below consists of five equal squares. The perimeter of the entire figure is 108 feet. What is the area the entire figure in square feet? [Area of a square or rectangle = Length × Width; Perimeter = (2 × Length) + (2 × Width)]

A) 45
B) 81
C) 324
D) 405
E) 540

Three sides of each of the exterior squares form the cross, so the cross has twelve sides. Get the length of one side of each square first. Then find the area of each square. Then multiply by the number of squares that makeup the figure.

The correct answer is D.

The entire figure has 12 sides, so divide 108 by 12 to get the length of one side:

$108 \div 12 = 9$

Then determine the area of each square. Remember that the area of a square or rectangle is length × width:

9 × 9 = 81

The figure consists of five squares, so multiply to solve:

81 × 5 = 405 square feet

50) A small circle has a radius of 5 inches, and a larger circle has a radius of 8 inches. What is the difference in inches between the circumferences of the two circles?
   A) 3
   B) 6
   C) 6π
   D) 9π
   E) 39π

> The question above is asking you to calculate the circumference of two circles. The formula for the circumference of a circle is:
>
> Circumference of a circle = $2\pi R$ = (2 × π × radius)
>
> Radius = diameter × $\frac{1}{2}$

The correct answer is C.

Use the formula from above: (2 × π × radius)

So, we calculate the circumference of the large circle as: 2 × π × 8 = 16π

The circumference of the small circle is: 2 × π × 5 = 10π

Then, we subtract to get our solution: $16\pi - 10\pi = 6\pi$

51) Which of the following statements about isosceles triangles is true?
   A) Isosceles triangles have two equal sides.
   B) When an altitude is drawn in an isosceles triangle, two equilateral triangles are formed.
   C) The base of an isosceles triangle must be shorter than the length of each of the other two sides.
   D) The sum of the measurements of the interior angles of an isosceles triangle must be equal to 360°.
   E) If two sides of an isosceles triangle are equal, the angles opposite them are right triangles.

This question assesses your knowledge of the rules for triangles and angles.

Remember these principles on angles and triangles for your exam:

The sum of all three angles in any triangle must be equal to 180 degrees.

An isosceles triangle has two equal sides and two equal angles.

An equilateral triangle has three equal sides and three equal angles.

Angles that have the same measurement in degrees are called congruent angles.

Equilateral triangles are sometimes called congruent triangles.

Two angles are supplementary if they add up to 180 degrees. This means that when the two angles are placed together, they will form a straight line on one side.

Two angles are complementary (sometimes called adjacent angles) if they add up to 90 degrees. This means that the two angles will form a right triangle.

A parallelogram is a four-sided figure in which opposite sides are parallel and equal in length. Each angle will have the same measurement as the angle opposite to it, so a parallelogram has two pairs of opposite angles.

The correct answer is A.

As stated above, an isosceles triangle has two equal sides, so answer A is correct.

If an altitude is drawn in an isosceles triangle, we have to put a straight line down the middle of the triangle from the peak to the base. Dividing the triangle in this way would form two right triangles, rather than two equilateral triangles. So, answer B is incorrect.

The base of an isosceles triangle can be longer than the length of each of the other two sides, so answer C is incorrect.

The sum of all three angles of any triangle must be 180 degrees, rather than 360 degrees. So, answer D is incorrect.

By definition a triangle must have three sides. Also remember that all three angles inside the triangle must add up to 180 degrees and that right angles measure 90 degrees.

Therefore, the angles opposite the two equal sides of an isosceles triangle cannot be right triangles because $2 \times 90° = 180°$. In this case, there would be no room for the third angle. So, answer E is incorrect.

52) Which of the following dimensions would be needed in order to find the area of the figure?

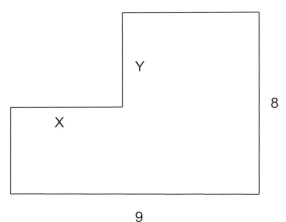

A) X only
B) Y only
C) Both X and Y
D) Either X or Y
E) Neither X nor Y

This question is asking you to calculate the area of a hybrid shape. To solve problems like this one, try to visualize two rectangles. The first rectangle would measure 8 × 9 and the second rectangle would measure X × Y.

The correct answer is C.

Essentially a rectangle is missing at the upper left-hand corner of the figure.

We would need to know both the length and width of the "missing" rectangle in order to calculate the area of our figure.

So, we need to know both X and Y in order to solve the problem.

53) The area of a square is 64 square units. This square is made up of smaller squares that measure 4 square units each. How many of the smaller squares are needed to make up the larger square?

A) 8
B) 12
C) 16
D) 24
E) 32

This question is asking you to determine the relationships between square figures of different sizes. For problems about placing small squares inside a larger square, you can simply divide the size of the smaller squares into the size of the larger square in order to determine how many small squares are required.

The correct answer is C.

We simply divide to get the answer: 64 ÷ 4 = 16

54) The illustration below shows an isosceles triangle. The entire triangle has a base of 9 and a height of 18.

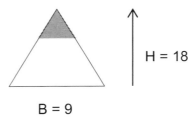

H = 18

B = 9

The shaded portion at the top of the triangle has a height of 6. What fraction expresses the area of the shaded portion to the area of the entire triangle?

State your answer as a fraction in the spaces provided.

Numerator value = _____

Denominator value = _____

This question is asking you to calculate the area of a triangle.

The formula for the area of a triangle is: $\frac{B \times H}{2}$

This can also be expressed as: (base × height) ÷ 2

The correct answers are a numerator of 9 and a denominator of 81.

Another possible answer is a numerator of 1 and a denominator of 9.

First, we need to calculate the area of the entire triangle:

$(9 \times 18) \div 2 = 81$

Then, we need to calculate the base of the shaded portion.

Since the height of the shaded portion is 6 and the height of the entire triangle is 18, we know by using the rules of similarity that the ratio of the base of the shaded portion to the base of the entire cone is $^6/_{18}$ or $^1/_3$.

Using this fraction, we can calculate the base for the shaded portion.

The base of the entire triangle is 9, so the base of the shaded portion is 3:

$9 \times \frac{1}{3} = 3$

Then, calculate the area of the shaded portion:

$(3 \times 6) \div 2 = 9$

So, we can express the volume of the shaded portion to the volume of the entire cone as: $\frac{9}{81}$

Alternatively, we can simplify this to $\frac{1}{9}$.

55) In the figure below, lines 1 and 2 are parallel. What is the measurement in degrees of angle y?

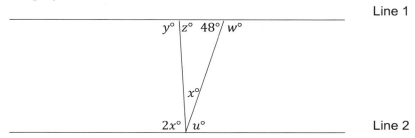

A) 48
B) 44
C) 88
D) 92
E) 132

When two parallel lines are cut by a transversal (a straight line that runs through or connects both of the parallel lines), opposite angles are formed. These opposite angles are equal in measure. In the illustration above, angle z and the angle that measures $2x°$ are opposite angles. Angle u and the 48° angle are also opposite angles.

The correct answer is D.

Because of the principles stated above, angle z measures $2x°$.

Remember that there are 180° degrees in total when we add up the three angles of any triangle and that two angles that form a straight line also add up to 180°.

So, we set up our equation for the triangle as follows: $180° = z° + x° + 48°$

We simplify this as shown:

$180° = z° + x° + 48°$
$180° = 2x° + x° + 48°$
$180° = 3x° + 48°$
$180° - 48° = 3x°$
$132° = 3x°$
$44° = x$

Then calculate the measurement of angle z:

$z° = 2x°$
$z° = 2 \times 44°$
$z = 88$

Finally, since $y° + z°$ forms a straight line and because straight lines measure 180°, we can calculate the measurement of angle y:

180° (for the straight line) − 88° (for angle z) = 92°

56) Consider rectangular figure WXYZ below:

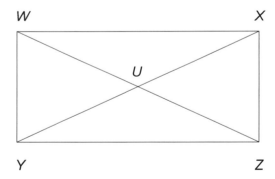

Which of the following must be true?
A) $\angle YWX \cong \angle YWU$
B) $\angle YUW \cong \angle WUX$
C) $\overline{WY} \cong \overline{UY}$
D) $\overline{WY} \cong \overline{WX}$
E) $\overline{WY} \cong \overline{XZ}$

Remember that opposite sides of a rectangle are equal in length. You may also wish to refer back to the rules on angles provided previously.

The correct answer is E.

$\overline{WY}$ and $\overline{XZ}$ are opposite sides of the rectangle, and opposite sides are equal in length.

The two opposite sides of a rectangle are also called corresponding sides.

Praxis Core Math Practice Set 2

For practice tests 2 and 3, you should refer to the formula sheet in the appendix of the book when needed.

1) Which of the following is the greatest?
   A) 0.540
   B) 0.054
   C) 0.045
   D) 0.5045
   E) 0.0054

2) Brooke wants to put new flooring in her living room. She will buy the flooring in square pieces that measure 1 square foot each. The entire room is 12 feet by 16 feet. The bookcases are one and a half feet deep from front to back. Flooring will not be put under the bookcases. Each piece of flooring costs $4.25. A diagram of her living room is provided.

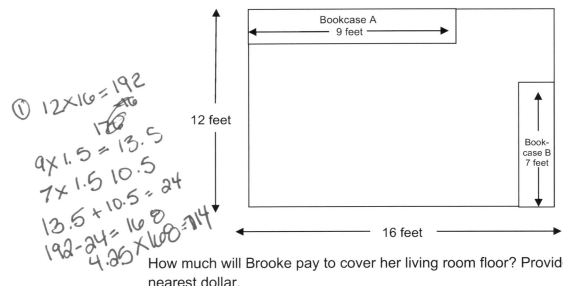

① 12×16=192
176
9×1.5 = 13.5
7×1.5 10.5
13.5 + 10.5 = 24
192-24 = 168
4.25 × 168 = 714

How much will Brooke pay to cover her living room floor? Provide the cost to the nearest dollar.
   A) 168
   B) 192
   C) 714
   D) 758
   E) 816

3) Farmer Brown has a field in which cows craze. He is going to buy fence panels to put up a fence along one side of the field. Each panel is 8 feet 6 inches long. He needs 11 panels to cover the entire side of the field. How long is the field?
A) 60 feet 6 inches
B) 72 feet 8 inches
C) 93 feet 6 inches
D) 102 feet 8 inches
E) 110 feet 6 inches

8"6

4) In the Venn diagram below, circle *A* represents the integers from 3 to 13 inclusive, and circle B represents the integers 5 to 15 inclusive. How many integers are represented in region C of the diagram?

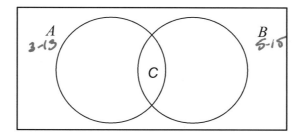

A) 2
B) 8
C) 9
D) 10
E) 11

5) If the value of x is between 0.0007 and 0.0021, which of the following could be x?
A) 0.0012
B) 0.0006
C) 0.0022
D) 0.022
E) 0.08

6) The total funds, represented by variable F, available for P charity projects is represented by the equation F = $500P + $3,700. If the charity has $40,000 available for projects, what is the greatest number of projects that can be completed?
A) 72
B) 73
C) 74
D) 79
E) 80

7) The students at Lyndon High School have been asked about their plans to attend the Homecoming Dance. The chart below shows the responses of each grade level by percentages. Which figure below best approximates the percentage of the total number of students from all four grades who will attend the dance? Note that each grade level has roughly the same number of students.

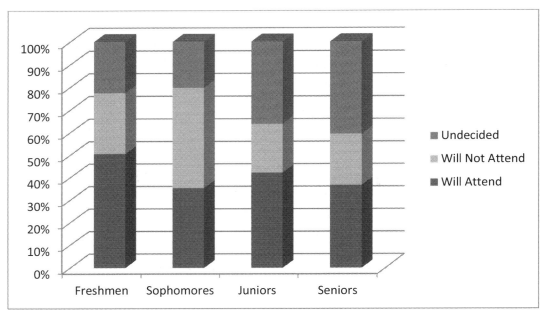

A) 25%
B) 35%
C) 45%
D) 55%
E) 60%

8) Look at the table below and answer the question that follows.

Sunday	Monday	Tuesday	Wednesday	Thursday	Friday	Saturday
−10°F	−9°F	1°F	6°F	8°F	13°F	12°F

What was the median temperature for the week?
A) 1°
B) 3°
C) 6°
D) 22°
E) 24°

9) During each flight, a flight attendant must count the number of passengers on board the aircraft. The morning flight had 52 passengers more than the evening flight, and there were 540 passengers in total on the two flights that day. How many passengers were there on the evening flight?

A) 244
B) 296
C) 488
D) 540
E) 592

10) A cafeteria serves spaghetti to senior citizens on Fridays. The spaghetti comes prepared in large containers, and each container holds 15 servings of spaghetti. The cafeteria is expecting 82 senior citizens this Friday. What is the least number of containers of spaghetti that the cafeteria will need in order to serve all 82 people?

A) 4
B) 5
C) 6
D) 7
E) 15

11) A caterpillar travels 10.5 inches in 45 seconds. How far will it travel in 6 minutes?

A) 45 inches
B) 63 inches
C) 64 inches
D) 84 inches
E) 90 inches

12) Which one of the values will correctly satisfy the following mathematical statement: $^2/_3 < ? < {}^7/_9$

A) $^1/_3$
B) $^1/_5$
C) $^2/_6$
D) $^1/_2$
E) $^7/_{10}$

13) Determine the ratio of side XZ to side WX in the figure below. Note that ΔUWX and ΔXYZ are similar.

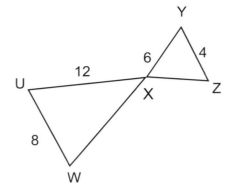

A) $\frac{3}{2}$

B) $\frac{2}{3}$

C) $\frac{4}{9}$

D) $\frac{9}{4}$

E) $\frac{1}{2}$

14) Which of the following are equivalent to 120,000,000? You may choose more than one answer.
A) 120 thousand thousands
B) 12 thousand thousands
C) 120 million
D) 120 billion

15) A company is making its budget for the cost of employees to attend conferences for the year. It costs $7,500 per year in total for the company plus C dollars per employee. During the year, the company has E employees. If the company has budgeted $65,000 for conference attendance, which equation can be used to calculate the maximum cost per employee?
A) ($65,000 − $7,500) ÷ E
B) ($65,000 − $7,500) ÷ C
C) (C − $7,500) ÷ E
D) $65,000 ÷ E
E) ($65,000 ÷ E) − $7,500

16) The pictograph below illustrates the results of a customer satisfaction survey by region. Each of the four regions has one salesperson. Salespeople in each region receive bonuses based on the amount of positive customer feedback they receive. If the salespeople from all four regions received $540 in bonuses in total, how much bonus money does the company pay each individual salesperson per satisfied customer?

Region 1	☺ ☺ ☺ ☺
Region 2	☺ ☺ ☺
Region 3	☺ ☺
Region 4	☺ ☺ ☺

Each ☺ represents positive feedback from 10 customers.

A) $4.00
B) $4.50
C) $4.90
D) $5.00
E) $5.40

17) A megastore gives away a cell phone for free to any customer who spends $2,250 or more in the store during the month of July. The store had $50,250 in total sales income for July, and 310 customers made purchases in the store during that month. Which equation below can be used to calculate the number of free cell phones that the store gave away during the month of July?
A) ($50,250 ÷ $2,250)
B) ($50,250 ÷ 310)
C) ($50,250 ÷ $2,250) ÷ 310
D) ($50,250 − $2,250) ÷ 310
E) Cannot be determined from the information provided.

18) Which of the following is equivalent to the expression $2(x + 2)(x − 3)$ for all values of x?
A) $2x^2 − 2x − 12$
B) $2x^2 − 10x − 6$
C) $2x^2 + 2x − 12$
D) $2x^2 + 10x − 6$
E) $2x^2 − x − 3$

19) A plumber charges $100 per job, plus $25 per hour worked. She is going to do 5 jobs this month. She will earn a total of $4,000. How many hours will she work this month? Please write your answer in the space provided.

_____ hours this month

20) What are two possible values of x for the following equation? $x^2 + 6x + 8 = 0$
A) 1 and 2
B) 2 and 4
C) 6 and 8
D) −2 and −4
E) −3 and −4

21) The ratio of teachers to students on a class trip is 2 to 6. Which of the following could possibly be the total number of teachers and students on the trip?
A) 90
B) 92
C) 94
D) 96
E) 98

22) A is 3 times B, and B is 3 more than 6 times C. Which of the following describes the relationship between A and C?
A) A is 9 more than 18 times C.
B) A is 3 more than 3 times C.
C) A is 3 more than 18 times C.
D) A is 6 more than 3 times C.
E) A is 18 more than 9 times C.

Go on to the next page.

23) The graph below shows the relationship between the number of days of rain per month and the amount of people who exercise outdoors per month. What relationship can be observed?

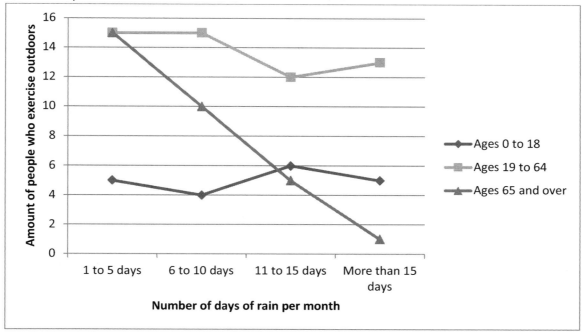

A) Young children are reliant upon an adult in order to exercise outdoors.
B) The exercise habits of working age people seem to fluctuate proportionately to the amount of rainfall.
C) In the 19 to 64 age group, there is a negative relationship between the number of days of rain and the amount of people who exercise outdoors.
D) People aged 65 and over seem less inclined to exercise outdoors when there is more rain.
E) No relationship can be observed because of the disparities inherent among the age groups.

24) A pharmacist works at a constant rate, filling 3 prescriptions every twenty minutes. How long will it take her to fill 45 prescriptions?
A) 1 hour 45 minutes
B) 2 hours 45 minutes
C) 4 hours 45 minutes
D) 5 hours
E) 6 hours 45 minutes

25) Consider the scatterplot below and then choose the best answer from the options that follow.

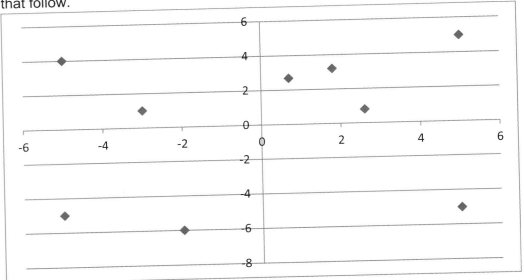

A) The scatterplot suggests a strong positive linear relationship between x and y.

B) The scatterplot suggests a strong negative linear relationship between x and y.

C) The scatterplot suggests a weak positive linear relationship between x and y.

D) The scatterplot suggests a weak negative linear relationship between x and y.

E) The scatterplot suggests that there is no relationship between x and y.

26) The graph of a line is shown on the xy plane below. The point that has the y-coordinate of 45 is not shown. What is the corresponding x-coordinate of that point?

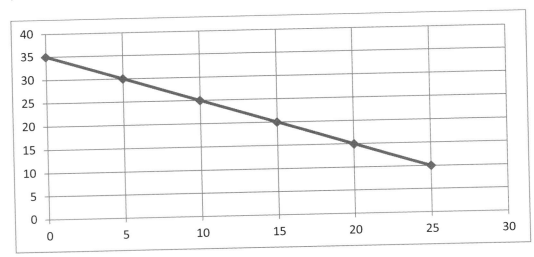

A) −10
B) −5
C) 0
D) 5
E) 30

27) Find the equivalent for the equation provided below.

$$\frac{x^5}{x^2 - 6x} + \frac{5}{x} = ?$$

A)

$$\frac{4 + x^6}{x^2 - 3x}$$

B)

$$\frac{4x^2 - 16x}{x^7}$$

C)

$$\frac{x^5 + 5x + 30}{x^2 - 6x}$$

D)

$$\frac{x^5 + 5x - 30}{x^2 + 6x}$$

E)

$$\frac{x^5 + 5x - 30}{x^2 - 6x}$$

28) One-half inch on a map represents *M* miles. Which of the following equations represents *M* + 5 miles on the map?

A) $\frac{M+5}{2M}$

B) $\frac{0.5M+2.5}{M}$

C) $\frac{2M+5}{M}$

D) $\frac{M+5}{2}$

E) $\frac{1}{2}M + 5$

29) Look at the table below and then answer the question that follows.

	Live in the City	Live in the Country
Factory workers	35	23
Office workers	42	20

The table above shows data on the distribution of residents of a particular county, according to their types of work and the locations of their residences. If one of the residents from this sample is selected at random, what is the probability that the resident will be an office worker who lives in the country?
A) $^1/_7$
B) $^1/_6$
C) $^1/_3$
D) $^{23}/_{120}$
E) $^{42}/_{120}$

30) Consider a data set of integers that are greater than 50 and less than 100? What is the range of numbers that are multiples of 5 in this data set?
A) 100
B) 50
C) 45
D) 40
E) 35

31) In a particular school, there are children with black hair, blonde hair, and brown hair. If one child is selected at random, the probability that the child has blonde hair is $1/6$ and the probability that the child has black hair is $3/4$. What is the probability that the child has brown hair?

A) $1/12$

B) $2/3$

C) $1/3$

D) $1/6$

E) $11/12$

32) The number of visitors a museum had on Tuesday (T) was twice as much as the number of visitors it had on Monday (M). The number of visitors it had on Wednesday (W) was 20% greater than that on Tuesday. Which equation can be used to calculate the total number of visitors to the museum for the three days?

A) W + .20W + 2T + M

B) 2M + T + W

C) M + 1.2T + W

D) M + 2T + W

E) 5.4M

33) A construction company is building new homes on a housing development. It has an agreement with the municipality that H number of houses must be built every 30 days. If H number of houses are not built during the 30-day period, the company has to pay a penalty to the municipality of P dollars per house. The penalty is paid per house for the number of houses that fall short of the 30-day target. If A represents the actual number of houses built during the 30-day period, which equation below can be used to calculate the penalty for the 30-day period?

A) $(H - P) \times 30$

B) $(H - A) \times P$

C) $(A - H) \times 30$

D) $(A - H) \times P$

E) $(H - A) \times 30$

34) The journey from Andersonville to Blairstown on the Regional Railway is always exactly the same duration. The journey times are shown in the table below.

Regional Railway Train Service from Andersonville to Blairstown	
Departure Time (Andersonville)	Arrival Time (Blairstown)
9:50 am	10:36 am
11:15 am	12:01 pm
12:30 pm	
2:15 pm	3:01 pm
	5:51 pm

What is the missing arrival time in Blairstown in the chart above?
A) 1:16 pm
B) 2:05 pm
C) 2:16 pm
D) 5:05 pm
E) 5:50 pm

35) Read the information below and then answer the question that follows.

- Tom and Mary are planning a cross-country trip.
- They plan to drive 300 miles each day for seven days.
- Their car can travel 25 miles on one gallon of gasoline.
- **Problem:** How much money in total will they need to pay for gasoline during their trip?

What piece of information is needed in order to answer the problem?
A) The amount of gasoline that the tank of the car can hold.
B) The total amount of miles that they will drive that week.
C) The price per gallon of gasoline.
D) The day of the week that their journey will begin.
E) No further information is required.

36) Use the diagram below to answer the question that follows.

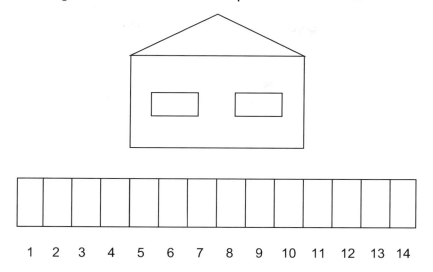

1   2   3   4   5   6   7   8   9   10   11   12   13   14

If each rectangle in the ruler below the picture of the house is one unit and the actual length of the house is 36 feet, then what is the scale of the diagram of the house?
A) 1 unit = 6 feet
B) 1 unit = 7.2 feet
C) 1 unit = 9 feet
D) 1 unit = 12 feet
E) 1 unit = 24 feet

37) A recipe of the ingredients needed to make 4 brownies is provided below.

Brownie recipe
¼ cup of flour
½ cup of sugar
¼ cup of butter
3 tablespoons of cocoa powder
¼ teaspoon of baking powder
½ teaspoon of vanilla extract

How much cocoa powder and baking powder together is needed to make 12 brownies? (1 tablespoon = 3 teaspoons)
A) 9¼ teaspoons
B) 9¾ teaspoons
C) 27¼ teaspoons
D) 27½ teaspoons
E) 27¾ teaspoons

38) Consider two concentric circles with radii of $R_1 = 1$ and $R_2 = 2.4$ as shown in the illustration below. Line L forms the diameter of the circles. What is the area of the lined part of the illustration?

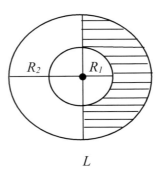

L

A) 0.7π
B) 1.4π
C) 2π
D) 2.38π
E) 2.8π

39) The illustration that follows represents a circular pond. The line from point X to point Y represents a bridge that passes over the exact center of the pond, and point X and Y lie on the circumference of the circle. The circumference of the pond is 176 yards. Approximately how long is the path in feet?

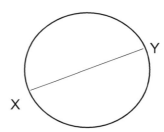

A) 28
B) 56
C) 58
D) 84
E) 168

40) The chart below shows data on the number of vehicles involved in accidents in Cedar Valley.

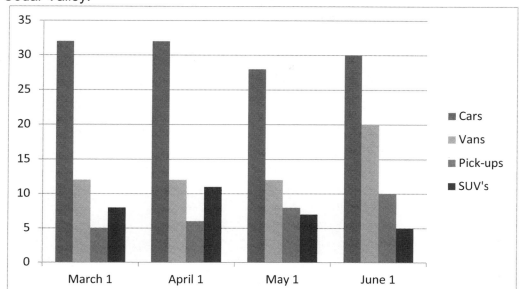

How many vans and SUV's were involved in accidents in Cedar Valley on March 1?

A) 15
B) 17
C) 20
D) 37
E) 39

41) Which of the following statements about parallelograms is true? You may select more than one response.

_____ (1) A parallelogram has no right angles.

_____ (2) A parallelogram has opposite angles which are congruent.

_____ (3) A parallelogram has two pairs of parallel sides.

_____ (4) The opposite sides of a parallelogram are unequal in measure.

_____ (5) A rectangle is not a parallelogram.

42) Which of the following statements best describes supplementary angles?
   A) Supplementary angles must add up to 90 degrees.
   B) Supplementary angles must add up to 180 degrees.
   C) Supplementary angles must add up to 360 degrees.
   D) Supplementary angles must be congruent angles.
   E) Supplementary angles must be opposite angles.

43) The area of a rectangle is 168 square units. This rectangle contains smaller rectangles that measure 2 square units each. How many of these small rectangles are needed to make up the entire rectangle?
   A)   13
   B)   28
   C)   42
   D)   84
   E) 168

44) Acme Packaging uses string to secure their packages prior to shipment. The string is tied around the entire length and entire width of the package, as shown in the following illustration:

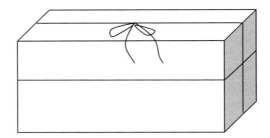

The box is ten inches in height, ten inches in depth, and twenty inches in length. An additional fifteen inches of string is needed to tie a bow on the top of the package. How much string is needed in total in order to tie up the entire package, including making the bow on the top?
   A)   40
   B)   80
   C) 100
   D) 120
   E) 135

45)   The triangle in the illustration below is an equilateral triangle. What is the measurement in degrees of angle a?

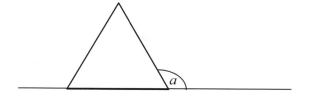

A) 40
B) 45
C) 60
D) 120
E) 130

46)   110 students took a math test. The mean score for the 60 female students was 95, while the mean score for the 50 male students was 90. Which figure below best approximates the mean test score for all 110 students in the class?
A) 55
B) 90
C) 92.5
D) 92.73
E) 95

47)   Carmen wanted to find the average of the five tests she has taken this semester. However, she erroneously divided the total points from the five tests by 4, which gave her a result of 90. What is the correct average of her five tests?
A) 72
B) 85
C) 86
D) 95
E) 112.5

48)   Return on investment (ROI) percentages are provided for seven companies. The ROI will be negative if the company operated at a loss, but the ROI will be a positive value if the company operated at a profit. The ROI's for the seven companies were: −2%, 5%, 7.5%, 14%, 17%, 1.3%, −3%. Which figure below best approximates the mean ROI for the seven companies?
A) 2%
B) 5.7%
C) 6.25%
D) 7.5%
E) 20%

49) A group of families had the following household incomes on their tax returns: $65000, $52000, $125000, $89000, $36000, $84000, $31000, $135000, $74000, and $87000. What is the range?

A) 74000
B) 77800
C) 79000
D) 84000
E) 104000

50) In an athletic competition, the maximum possible number of points was 25 points per participant. The scores for 15 different participants are displayed in the graph below. What was the median score for the 15 participants?

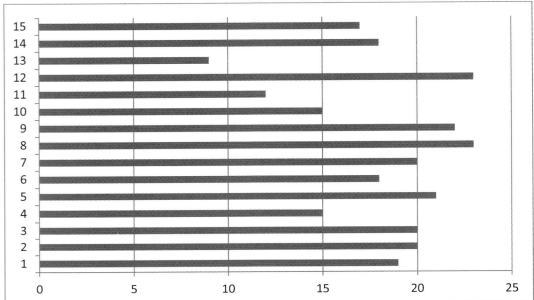

A) 15
B) 17
C) 18
D) 19
E) 23

51) A jar contains 4 red marbles, 6 green marbles, and 10 white marbles. If a marble is drawn from the jar at random, what is the probability that this marble is white?

A) $^1/_2$
B) $^1/_5$
C) $^1/_{10}$
D) $^3/_{10}$
E) $^9/_{20}$

52) Which of these numbers cannot be a probability? (There is more than one answer.)
A) −0.02
B) 0
C) 1.002
D) 1
E) $^1/_4$

53) An electricity company measures the energy consumption for each home in kilowatt hours (KWH). During July, the homes in one street had the levels of consumption in KWH in the chart show below. What is the mode of the level of energy consumption for this neighborhood for July?

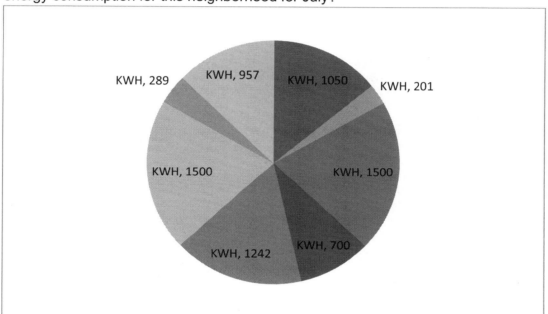

A) 700
B) 957
C) 828.5
D) 929.875
E) 1500

54) A die is rolled and a coin is tossed. What is the probability that the die shows an even number and the coin shows tails?

A) $^1/_2$

B) $^1/_4$

C) $^1/_6$

D) $^1/_{12}$

E) $^1/_{24}$

55) The blood types of 100 donors are shown in the following chart. If a donation from this group of donors is selected at random, what is the probability that type AB blood will be selected?

Blood Type	Number of donors
A positive	10
A negative	12
B positive	18
B negative	20
O type	25
AB type	15

A) $^{15}/_{99}$

B) $^{14}/_{100}$

C) $^3/_{20}$

D) $^1/_4$

E) $^3/_5$

56) A family is planning an annual picnic in Arizona. Rain is forecast for 45 days of the year, but when rain is forecast, the prediction is correct only 90% of the time. What is the probability that it will rain on the day of the picnic? Note that it is not a leap year.

A) 2.2222%

B) 11.0959%

C) 12.3288%

D) 45%

E) 90%

Praxis Core Math Practice Set 2 – Answer Key

1) A

2) C

3) C

4) C

5) A

6) A

7) B

8) C

9) A

10) C

11) D

12) E

13) E

14) A and C

15) A

16) B

17) E

18) A

19) 140 hours

20) D

21) D

22) A

23) D

24) D

25) E

26) A

27) E

28) B

29) B

30) D

31) A

32) E

33) B

34) A

35) C

36) A

37) E

38) D

39) E

40) C

41) (2) and (3)

42) B

43) D

44) E

45) D

46) D

47) A

48) B

49) E

50) D

51) A

52) A and C

53) E

54) B

55) C

56) B

Praxis Core Math Practice Set 2 – Solutions and Explanations

1) The correct answer is A. For problems with decimals, line the figures up in a column and add zeroes to fill in the column as shown below:

0.5400

0.0540

0.0450

0.5045

0.0054

If you still struggle with decimals, you can remove the decimal points and the zeroes before the other integers in order to see the answer more clearly.

0.5400

0.0540

0.0450

0.5045

0.0054

When we have removed the zeroes in front of the other numbers, we can see that the largest number is the first one, which is 0.54.

2) The correct answer is C. Calculate the total square footage of the room first: $12 \times 16 = 192$ total square feet. Then calculate the area under each bookcase. Bookcase A: $9 \times 1.5 = 13.5$; Bookcase B: $7 \times 1.5 = 10.5$; Total bookcase area: $13.5 + 10.5 = 24$ square feet. Next find the area of the room without the bookcase area: $192 - 24 = 168$ square feet to be covered. Finally, determine the cost: 168 square feet × \$4.25 per piece = \$714 total cost

3) The correct answer is C. Each panel is 8 feet 6 inches long, and he needs 11 panels to cover the entire side of the field. So, we need to multiply 8 feet 6 inches by 11, and then simplify the result. Step 1: 8 feet × 11 = 88 feet; Step 2: 6 inches × 11 = 66 inches; Step 3: There are 12 inches in a foot, so we need to determine how many feet and inches there are in 66 inches. 66 inches ÷ 12 = 5 feet 6 inches; Step 4: Now add the two results together. 88 feet + 5 feet 6 inches = 93 feet 6 inches

4) The correct answer is C. Circle A contains these numbers: 3, 4, 5, 6, 7, 8, 9, 10, 11, 12, 13. Circle B contains these numbers: 5, 6, 7, 8, 9, 10, 11, 12, 13, 14, 15. Now

look to see which numbers are included in both data sets for region C. 5, 6, 7, 8, 9, 10, 11, 12, 13 are included in both sets. So, region C contains 9 numbers.

5) The correct answer is A. This problem is like question 1 above, except here we need to find a missing value. Remember to put in zeroes and line up the decimal points when you compare the numbers.

   0.0007

   A. 0.0012

   B. 0.0006

   C. 0.0022

   D. 0.0220

   E. 0.0800

   0.0021

   Answer choice B is less than 0.0007, and answer choices C, D, and E are greater than 0.0021. Answer choice A (0.0012) is between 0.0007 and 0.0021, so it is the correct answer.

6) The correct answer is A. The equation is: F = $500P + $3,700. We are told that the total funds are $40,000 so put that in the equation to solve the problem.

   $40,000 = $500P + $3,700

   $40,000 − $3,700 = $500P

   $36,300 = $500P

   $36,300 ÷ 500 = $500 ÷ 500P

   $36,300 ÷ 500 = 72.6

   Since a fraction of a project cannot be undertaken, the greatest number of projects is 72.

7) The correct answer is B. The dark gray part at the bottom of each bar represents those students who will attend the dance. 45% of the freshman, 30% of the sophomores, 38% of the juniors, and 30% of the seniors will attend. Calculating the average, we get the overall percentage for all four grades: (45 + 30 + 38 + 30) ÷ 4 = 35.75%.

   35% is the closest answer to 35.75%, so it best approximates our result.

8) The correct answer is C. Place the values for the temperatures in ascending order: −10, −9, 1, 6, 8, 12, 13. The median is in the middle: −10, −9, 1 , **6** , 8, 12, 13

9) The correct answer is A. The problem tells us that the morning flight had 52 passengers more than the evening flight, and there were 540 passengers in total on the two flights that day. Step 1: First of all, we need to deduct the difference from the total: 540 − 52 = 488; In other words, there were 488 passengers on both flights combined, plus the 52 additional passengers on the morning flight. Step 2: Now divide this result by 2 to allocate an amount of passengers to each flight: 488 ÷ 2 = 244 passengers on the evening flight. Had the question asked you for the number of passengers on the morning flight, you would have had to add back the number of additional passengers to find the total amount of passengers for the morning flight: 244 + 52 = 296 passengers on the morning flight

10) The correct answer is C. Divide and then round up: 82 people in total ÷ 15 people served per container = 5.467 containers. We need to round up to 6 since we cannot purchase a fractional part of a container.

11) The correct answer is D. The question is asking us about a time duration of 6 minutes, so we need to calculate the amount of seconds in 6 minutes: 6 minutes × 60 seconds per minute = 360 seconds in total. Then divide the total time by the amount of time needed to make one journey: 360 seconds ÷ 45 seconds per journey = 8 journeys. Finally, multiply the number of journeys by the amount of inches per journey in order to get the total inches: 10.5 inches for 1 journey × 8 journeys = 84 inches in total

12) The correct answer is E. First of all, we need to find a common denominator for the fractions in the inequality, as well as for the fractions in the answer choices. In order to complete the problem quickly, you should not try to find the lowest common denominator, but just find any common denominator. We can do this by expressing all of the numbers with a denominator of 90, since 9 is the largest denominator in the equation and 10 is the largest denominator in the answer choices.

$\frac{2}{3} \times \frac{30}{30} = \frac{60}{90}$

$\frac{7}{9} \times \frac{10}{10} = \frac{70}{90}$

Then, express the original equation in terms of the common denominator:

$\frac{60}{90} < ? < \frac{70}{90}$

Next, convert the answer choices to the common denominator.

A. $\frac{1}{3} \times \frac{30}{30} = \frac{30}{90}$

B. $\frac{1}{5} \times \frac{18}{18} = \frac{18}{90}$

C. $\frac{2}{6} \times \frac{15}{15} = \frac{30}{90}$

D. $\frac{1}{2} \times \frac{45}{45} = \frac{45}{90}$

E. $\frac{7}{10} \times \frac{9}{9} = \frac{63}{90}$

Finally, compare the results to find the answer. By comparing the numerators (the top numbers of the fractions), we can see that $\frac{63}{90}$ lies between $\frac{60}{90}$ and $\frac{70}{90}$. So, E is the correct answer because $\frac{60}{90} < \frac{63}{90} < \frac{70}{90}$.

13) The correct answer is E. In ΔXYZ the long side of the triangle is 6 and ΔUWX the long side is 12. So, the ratio of the triangles is 6:12, which we simplify to 1:2 or $\frac{1}{2}$. The ratios for the two other corresponding sides are the same because the triangles are similar. So, the ratio of the other sides must also be 1:2 or $\frac{1}{2}$.

14) The correct answers are A and C. A number with seven to nine figures is in the millions. Here our number ends in zeros, so we can clearly see that a number with six zeros in the last six places of the number is in the millions. A million is equal to a thousand thousands. So, the correct answers are 120 million and 120 thousand thousands.

15) The correct answer is A. The total amount of the budget is $65,000. The up-front cost is $7,500, so we can determine the remaining amount of available funds by deducting the up-front cost from the total: $65,000 – $7,500. We have to divide the available amount by the number of employees (E) to get the maximum cost per employee: ($65,000 – $7,500) ÷ E

16) The correct answer is B. First of all, add up the number of faces on the chart: 4 + 3 + 2 + 3 = 12 faces. Each face represents 10 customers, so multiply to get the total number of customers: 12 × 10 = 120 customers in total for all four regions. The salespeople received $540 in total, so we need to divide this by the number of customers: $540 ÷ 120 customers = $4.50 per customer

17) The correct answer is E. We cannot determine the information because we would need to know exactly how much each individual customer spent in order to determine whether or not the particular customer received a free gift. We cannot simply divide and use the average.

18) The correct answer is A. The FOIL method is used on polynomials, which are equations that look like this: $(a + b)(c + d)$

You multiply the variables or terms in the parentheses in this order:

First Inside Outside Last

We can use the FOIL method on our example equation as follows:

$(a + b)(c + d) =$

$(a \times c) + (a \times d) + (b \times c) + (b \times d) =$

$ac + ad + bc + bd$

You should use the FOIL method in this problem. Be very careful with the negative numbers when doing the multiplication.

$2(x + 2)(x - 3) =$

$2[(x \times x) + (x \times -3) + (2 \times x) + (2 \times -3)] =$

$2(x^2 + -3x + 2x + -6) =$

$2(x^2 - 3x + 2x - 6) =$

$2(x^2 - x - 6)$

Then multiply each term by the 2 at the front of the parentheses.

$2(x^2 - x - 6) =$

$2x^2 - 2x - 12$

19) The correct answer is 140 hours. The plumber is going to earn $4,000 for the month. She charges a set fee of $100 per job, and she will do 5 jobs, so we can calculate the total set fees first: $100 set fee per job × 5 jobs = $500 total set fees. Then deduct the set fees from the total for the month in order to determine the total for the hourly pay: $4,000 – $500 = $3,500. She earns $25 per hour, so divide the hourly rate into the total hourly pay in order to determine the number of hours she will work: $3,500 total hourly pay ÷ $25 per hour = 140 hours to work

20) The correct answer is D.

Substitute values for x to solve.

For x = –2

$x^2 + 6x + 8 = 0$

$-2^2 + (6 \times -2) + 8 = 0$

$4 - 12 + 8 = 0$

The above statement is correct, so x = –2 is one possible value.

For x = –4

$x^2 + 6x + 8 = 0$

$-4^2 + (6 \times -4) + 8 = 0$

$16 - 24 + 8 = 0$

The above statement is also correct, so x = –4 is the other possible value.

21) The correct answer is D. For questions on ratios, your first step is usually going to be to add the two parts of the ratio together: 2 + 6 = 8. So, we know that the total will have to be divisible by 8 in order to keep the total in proportion. Answer D (96) is the only answer choice that meets this criterion since 96 ÷ 8 = 12.

22) The correct answer is A. The problem tells us that A is 3 times B, and B is 3 more than 6 times C. So, we need to create equations based on this information.

B is 3 more than 6 times C: B = 6C + 3

A is 3 times B: A = 3B

Since B = 6C + 3, we can substitute 6C + 3 for B in the second equation as follows:

A = 3B

A = 3(6C + 3)

A = 18C + 9

So, A is 9 more than 18 times C.

23) The correct answer is D. The most striking relationship on the graph is the line for ages 65 and over, which clearly shows a negative relationship between exercising outdoors and the number of days of rain per month. You will recall that a negative relationship exists when an increase in one variable causes a decrease in the other variable. So, we can conclude that people aged 65 and over seem less inclined to exercise outdoors when there is more rain.

24) The correct answer is D. Divide the 45 total prescriptions by the amount stated in the rate (3 prescriptions): 45 ÷ 3 = 15. Then multiply this amount by the time stated in the rate (20 minutes) to solve: 15 × 20 = 300 minutes. Finally express in hours, if possible: 300 minutes ÷ 60 minutes per hour = 5 hours

25) The correct answer is E. When looking at scatterplots, try to see if the dots are roughly grouped into any kind of pattern or line. If so, positive or negative relationships may be represented. Here, however, the dots are located at what

appear to be random places in all four quadrants of the graph. So, the scatterplot suggests that there is no relationship between x and y.

26) The correct answer is A. As x decreases by 5, y increases by 5. So, if we want to determine the x coordinate for $(x, 45)$ we need to deduct 10 from the x coordinate of $(0, 35)$. Therefore, the coordinates are $(-10, 45)$, and the answer is -10.

27) The correct answer is E. Find the lowest common denominator. Since x is common to both denominators, we can convert the denominator of the second fraction to the LCD by multiplying by $(x - 6)$.

$$\frac{x^5}{x^2 - 6x} + \frac{5}{x} =$$

$$\frac{x^5}{x^2 - 6x} + \left(\frac{5}{x} \times \frac{x - 6}{x - 6}\right) =$$

$$\frac{x^5}{x^2 - 6x} + \frac{5x - 30}{x^2 - 6x} =$$

$$\frac{x^5 + 5x - 30}{x^2 - 6x}$$

28) The correct answer is B. The ratio of 0.5 inch for M miles can be represented mathematically as $\frac{0.5}{M}$. The ratio for $M + 5$ is not known, so we can represent the unknown as x: $\frac{x}{M+5}$. Finally, use cross multiplication to solve the problem:

$$\frac{0.5}{M} = \frac{x}{M+5}$$

$$0.5 \times (M + 5) = Mx$$

Then divide by M to isolate x and solve the problem.

$$[0.5 \times (M + 5)] \div M = Mx \div M$$

$$\frac{0.5M + 2.5}{M} = x$$

29) The correct answer is B. First add up all of the amounts to get the total amount: $35 + 42 + 23 + 20 = 120$. We divide the number of office workers who live in the country, which is 20 people, into this total to get our answer. We can find this amount in the lower right-hand corner of the chart. So, set up the fraction and then simplify: $20 \div 120 = {}^{20}/_{120} = {}^{2}/_{12} = {}^{1}/_{6}$

81

30) The correct answer is D. The question is asking us for numbers greater than 50 and less than 100. The number 55 is the first multiple of 5 that is greater than 5, and 95 is the first multiple of 5 that is less than 100. The range is the difference between two numbers, found by subtracting the lower number from the higher number. So, subtract to solve: $95 - 55 = 40$

31) The correct answer is A. Find the lowest common denominator on the fractions. Here our common denominator is 12. For the children with blonde hair, the fraction with the common denominator is: $^1/_6 \times {}^2/_2 = {}^2/_{12}$ and for the children with black hair, it is $^3/_4 \times {}^3/_3 = {}^9/_{12}$. Then add these amounts together: $^2/_{12} + {}^9/_{12} = {}^{11}/_{12}$. The rest of the children have brown hair. The entire class is represented by the fraction $^{12}/_{12}$, so subtract to solve: $^{12}/_{12} - {}^{11}/_{12} = {}^1/_{12}$

32) The correct answer is E. Set up each part of the problem as an equation. The museum had twice as many visitors on Tuesday (T) as on Monday (M), so T = 2M. The number of visitors on Wednesday exceeded that of Tuesday by 20%, so W = 1.20 × T. Then express T in terms of M for Wednesday's visitors: W = 1.20 × T = 1.20 × 2M = 2.40M. Finally, add the amounts together for all three days: M + 2M + 2.40M = 5.4M

33) The correct answer is B. First, we need to calculate the shortage in the number of houses actually built. If H represents the number of houses that should be built and A represents the actual number of houses built, then the shortage is calculated as: $H - A$. The company has to pay P dollars per house for the shortage, so we calculate the total penalty by multiplying the shortage by the penalty per house: $(H - A) \times P$

34) The correct answer is A. Each journey lasts 46 minutes, so if the train departs at 12:30 pm, it will arrive at 1:16 pm. (12:30 + 46 minutes = 1:16)

35) The correct answer is C. In order to solve this problem, we would need to multiply the number of gallons of gasoline used each day by the cost of gasoline per gallon to calculate the cost per day. We would then add the daily amounts together to get the total cost during their entire trip. From these required facts, we are lacking the price of gasoline per gallon.

36) The correct answer is A. Count the number of units that the house spans, rather than trying to subtract units from the total of 14. If we count the number of units below the house in the drawing, we can see that the house spans 6 units. Divide this result into the actual length of the house (36 feet) to get the scale of the drawing. 36 feet ÷ 6 units = 6 feet represented by each unit

37) The correct answer is E. 3 tablespoons of cocoa powder and ¼ teaspoon of baking powder are needed for the original recipe to make 4 brownies. There are 3 teaspoons in a tablespoon, so calculate the total teaspoons needed for the original recipe first: 3 tablespoons × 3 = 9 teaspoons cocoa powder + ¼ teaspoon baking powder = 9¼ teaspoons in total. We are now making 12 brownies, so we need to multiply all of the ingredients by 3: 9¼ × 3 = 27¾ teaspoons

38) The correct answer is D. The circles are concentric, meaning that they share the same center. The formula for the area of a circle is: $\pi \times R^2$. First, we need to calculate the area of the larger circle: $\pi \times 2.4^2 = 5.76\pi$. Then calculate the area of the smaller inner circle: $\pi \times 1^2 = \pi$. We need to find the difference between half of each circle, so divide the area of each circle by 2 and then subtract:

$$(5.76\pi \div 2) - (\pi \div 2) = \frac{5.76\pi}{2} - \frac{\pi}{2} = \frac{4.76\pi}{2} = 2.38\pi$$

39) The correct answer is E. For this question, you need the formula for the circumference of a circle: $\pi \times$ diameter = circumference. If you do not see π in any of the answer choices, use 3.14 for π to solve. We are given the circumference, so we need to divide the circumference by π or 3.14 to get the diameter in yards: 176 ÷ 3.14 = 56.05, which we round down to 56 yards. There are three feet in a yard, so multiply to get the final answer: 56 × 3 = 168

40) The correct answer is C. Vans were involved in 12 accidents on March 1, and SUV's were involved in 8 accidents on the same date. So, vans and SUV's had 20 accidents in total on this date.

41) The correct answers are (2) and (3). A parallelogram is a four-sided figure that has two pairs of parallel sides. The opposite or facing sides of a parallelogram are of equal length and the opposite angles of a parallelogram are of equal measure. You will recall that congruent is another word for equal in measure. So, answers 2 and 3 are correct. A rectangle is a parallelogram with four angles of equal size (all of which are right angles), while a square is a parallelogram with four sides of equal length and four right angles.

42) The correct answer is B. Two angles are supplementary if they add up to 180 degrees.

43) The correct answer is D. A rectangle consisting of 2 square units will look like the following illustration: ⬜⬜

So, we divide the total number of squares in the larger rectangle by 2: 168 ÷ 2 = 84

44) The correct answer is E. The string that goes around the front, back, and sides of the package is calculated as follows: 20 + 10 + 20 + 10 = 60. The string that goes around the top, bottom, and sides of the package is calculated in the same way since the top and bottom are equal in length to the front and back: 20 + 10 + 20 + 10 = 60. So, 120 inches of string is needed so far. Then, we need 15 extra inches for the bow: 120 + 15 = 135

45) The correct answer is D. An equilateral triangle has three equal sides and three equal angles. Since all 3 angles in any triangle need to add up to 180 degrees, each angle of an equilateral triangle is 60 degrees (180 ÷ 3 = 60). Angles that lie along the same side of a straight line must add up to 180. So, we calculate angle a as follows: 180 − 60 = 120

46) The correct answer is D. You need to find the total points for all the females and the total points for all the males: Females: 60 × 95 = 5700; Males: 50 × 90 = 4500. Then add these two amounts together and divide by the total number of students in the class to get your solution: (5700 + 4500) ÷ 110 = 10,200 ÷ 110 = 92.73 average for all 110 students

47) The correct answer is A. First you need to find the total points that the student earned. You do this by taking Carmen's erroneous average times 4: 4 × 90 = 360. Then divide the total points earned by the correct number of tests in order to get the correct average: 360 ÷ 5 = 72

48) The correct answer is B. The mean is the arithmetic average. First, add up all of the items: −2% + 5% + 7.5% + 14% + 17% + 1.3% + −3% = 39.8%. Then divide by 7 since there are 7 companies in the set: 39.8% ÷ 7 = 5.68% ≈ 5.7%

49) The correct answer is E. The range is the highest number minus the lowest number. Our data set is: $65000, $52000, $125000, $89000, $36000, $84000, $31000, $135000, $74000, and $87000. So, the range is: $135000 − $31000 = $104000

50) The correct answer is D. The median is the number that is halfway through the set. Reading the graph from the bottom to top, our data set is: 19, 20, 20, 15, 21, 18, 20, 23, 22, 15, 12, 23, 9, 18, 17. First, put the numbers in ascending order: 9, 12, 15, 15, 17, 18, 18, 19, 20, 20, 20, 21, 22, 23, 23. We have 15 numbers, so the 8th number in the set is halfway and is therefore the median:

9, 12, 15, 15, 17, 18, 18, **19**, 20, 20, 20, 21, 22, 23, 23

51) The correct answer is A. Your first step is to calculate the total amount of items in the data set: 4 red marbles + 6 green marbles + 10 white marbles = 20 marbles in total. The probability is expressed with the subset in the numerator and the total

remaining data set in the denominator. So, the chance of drawing a white marble is:

$^{10}/_{20} = ^{1}/_{2}$

52) The correct answers are A and C. Probability will be 1 for a 100% probability, 0 for something that has no change of occurring, or a positive number less than 1 for all other probabilities. Probability can be expressed as a decimal or a fraction. Probability therefore cannot be a negative number or a number greater than 1.

53) The correct answer is E. The mode is the number in the set that occurs most frequently. Our data set is: 1050, 201, 1500, 700, 1242, 1500, 289, 957. The number 1500 is the only number that occurs more than once, so it is the mode.

54) The correct answer is B. The data set can be expressed as follows:

(1,H),(2,H),(3,H),(4,H),(5,H),(6,H), (1,T),(2,T),(3,T),(4,T),(5,T),(6,T)

Counting the items in the above set, we can see that there are 12 items in total.

The desired outcome is that the die shows an even number and the coin shows tails.

The possible outcomes are: {(2,T),(4,T),(6,T)}

So, the probability is: $^{3}/_{12} = ^{1}/_{4}$

55) The correct answer is C. The total for the data set is: 10 + 12 + 18 + 20 + 25 + 15 = 100. There are 15 donors with type AB blood, so the probability is $^{15}/_{100} = ^{3}/_{20}$

56) The correct answer is B. The event is defined as the chance of rain. In terms of probabilities, we know that there are 365 days in non-leap years, so this goes in the denominator. The chance of rain goes in the numerator: $^{45}/_{365} = 12.3288\%$.

However, the forecast is correct only 90% of the time: $12.3288\% \times 90\% = 11.0959\%$

Praxis Core Math Practice Set 3

1)   Pilar does the following calculation:

10 kilometers × 1000 meters/1 kilometer × 100 centimeters/1 meter

What conversion is she doing?
A) Meters to kilometers
B) Centimeters to meters
C) Kilometers to meters
D) Kilometers to centimeters
E) Centimeters to kilometers

2)   Which of the following shows the numbers ordered from least to greatest?
A) 0.2135
      0.3152
      0.0253
      0.0012

B) 0.3152
      0.2135
      0.0253
      0.0012

C) 0.0253
      0.0012
      0.3152
      0.2135

D) 0.0012
      0.0253
      0.2135
      0.3152

E) 0.3152
      0.2135
      0.0012
      0.0253

3) If $\frac{x}{24}$ is between 8 and 9, which of the following could be the value of x?
   A) 190
   B) 191
   C) 200
   D) 217
   E) 220

4) The ratio of bags of apples to bags of oranges in a particular grocery store is 2 to 3. If there are 44 bags of apples in the store, how many bags of oranges are there?
   A) 33
   B) 48
   C) 55
   D) 63
   E) 66

5) Ali uses a jar of coffee every 7 days. Approximately how many jars of coffee will he need to last the entire year?
   A) 48
   B) 50
   C) 52
   D) 54
   E) 55

6) At the beginning of class, $^1/_5$ of the students leave to go to singing lessons. Then $^1/_4$ of the remaining students leave to go to the principal's office. If 18 students are then left in the class, how many students were there at the beginning of class?
   A) 90
   B) 45
   C) 30
   D) 25
   E) 24

7) In the last step of doing a calculation, Wei Li added 92 instead of subtracting 92. What shortcut can Wei Li perform in order to get the correct calculation?
   A) Subtract 46 from his erroneous result.
   B) Add 92 to his erroneous result.
   C) Subtract 92 from his erroneous result.
   D) Add 184 to his erroneous result.
   E) Subtract 184 from his erroneous result.

8) Chantelle took a test that had four parts. The total number of questions on each part is given in the table below, as is the number of questions that Chantelle answered correctly.

Part	Total Number of Questions	Number of Questions Answered Correctly
1	15	12
2	25	20
3	35	32
4	45	32

Which fraction below best represents the relationship of Chantelle's incorrect answers on Part 1 to the total points on Part 1?
A) 1/5
B) 1/3
C) 4/5
D) 4/6
E) 5/6

9) A dance academy had 300 students at the beginning of January. It lost 5% of its students during the month. However, 15 new students joined the academy on the last day of the month. If this pattern continues for the next two months, how many students will there be at the academy at the end of March?
A) 285
B) 300
C) 310
D) 315
E) 320

10) In a group of children, one-half have had a tetanus shot. Of that half, only one-third suffered wounds that would have caused tetanus. In which of the following graphs does the dark gray area represent that third of the group?

A)

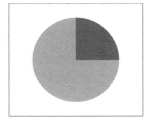

B)

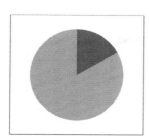

C)

D)

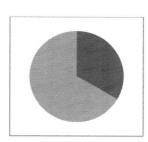

E)

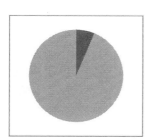

11) The residents of Hendersonville took a census. As part of the census, each resident had to indicate how many relatives they had living within a ten-mile radius of the town. The results of that particular question on the census are represented in the graph below.

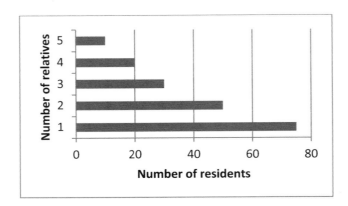

How many residents of Hendersonville had more than 3 relatives living within a ten-mile radius of the town?
A)   10
B)   20
C)   30
D) 155
E) 175

12) In the isosceles triangle RST shown below, angle T is congruent to angle R. If angle T is 49° , what is the measurement in degrees of angle S?

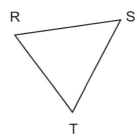

A) 49
B) 82
C) 98
D) 108
E) 131

13) A motorcycle traveled 38.4 miles in $^4/_5$ of an hour. What was the speed of the motorcycle in miles per hour?
A) 9.6
B) 30.72
C) 48
D) 52
E) 60

14) A factory that makes microchips produces 20 times as many functioning chips as defective chips. If the factory produced 11,235 chips in total last week, how many of them were defective?
A) 535
B) 561
C) 1,070
D) 10,700
E) 11,215

15) A town has recently suffered a flood. The total cost, represented by variable C, which is available to accommodate R number of residents in emergency housing is represented by the equation C = $750R + $2,550. If the town has a total of $55,000 available for emergency housing, what is the greatest number of residents that it can house?
A) 68
B) 69
C) 70
D) 71
E) 75

16) The numbers in the following list are ordered from least to greatest:
α , $^2/_7$, $^8/_9$, 1.35, $^{11}/_3$, μ
Which of the following could be the value of μ? Be sure to choose all possible answers.
A) 3.5
B) $^{10}/_4$
C) 4.1
D) $^1/_6$
E) $^3/_7$

17) The pictograph below shows the number of traffic violations that occur every week in a certain city. The fine for speeding violations is $50 per violation. The fine for other violations is $20 per violation. The total collected for all three types of violations was $6,000. What is the fine for each parking violation?

Speeding	☆ ☆
Parking	☆
Other violations	☆ ☆ ☆

Each ☆ represents 30 violations.

A) $20
B) $30
C) $40
D) $100
E) $140

18) Sam is driving a truck at 70 miles per hour. He will drive through four towns on his route: Brownsville, Dunnstun, Farnam, and Georgetown. At 10:30 am, he sees this sign:

Brownsville	35 miles
Dunnstun	70 miles
Farnam	140 miles
Georgetown	210 miles

He continues driving at the same speed. What time will Sam arrive in Georgetown if he takes a 30-minute break in Farnam?
A) 1:00 pm
B) 1:30 pm
C) 2:00 pm
D) 2:30 pm
E) 2:45 pm

19)   Look at the pie chart below and answer the question that follows.

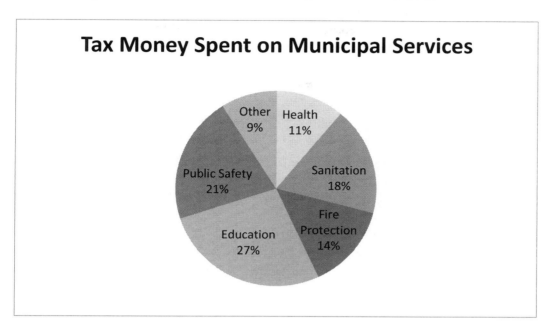

Tax Money Spent on Municipal Services

For next year, $6,537,200 in total tax money is budgeted for all municipal services. Each category is allocated the same percentage of next year's budget as the actual percentage spent for the current year. What is the budget amount for public safety?
A) $915,208
B) $1,107,813
C) $1,372,812
D) $1,765,004
E) $1,765,040

20)   Look at the data below about a martial arts class and answer the question that follows.

There are 53 students at the beginning of the year.
• 15 students have black belts
• 22 have brown belts
• 8 have blue belts
• 8 have belts of other colors

At the end of the year:
• 3 of the students with brown belts have dropped out of the class
• 2 of the students with belts of other colors have also dropped out of the class
• 4 new students have joined the class

Which of the following facts can be determined from the information provided?
A) The total number of students in the class.
B) The number of students in the class with brown belts.
C) The number of students in the class with blue belts.
D) The number of students in the class with black belts.
E) No facts can be determined since there is not sufficient information.

21) The price of a sofa at a local furniture store was x dollars on Wednesday this week. On Thursday, the price of the sofa was reduced by 10% of Wednesday's price. On Friday, the price of the sofa was reduced again by 15% of Thursday's price. Which of the following expressions can be used to calculate the price of the sofa on Friday?
A) $(0.25)x$
B) $(0.75)x$
C) $(0.10)(0.15)x$
D) $(0.10)(0.85)x$
E) $(0.90)(0.85)x$

22) Each square in the diagram below is one yard wide and one yard long. The gray area of the diagram represents New Town's water reservoir. The white area represents the surrounding conservation park.

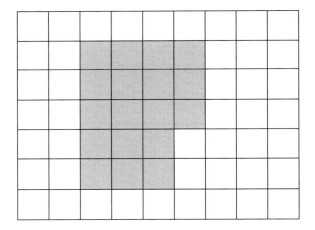

Which of the following ratios represents the area of the reservoir to the area of the surrounding conservation park?
A) 2:5
B) 9:23
C) 17:32
D) 18:44
E) 32:17

23) There are three boys in a family, named Alex, Burt, and Zander. Alex is twice as old as Burt, and Burt is one year older than three times the age of Zander. Which of the following statements best describes the relationship between the ages of the boys?
A) Alex is 4 years older than 6 times the age of Zander.
B) Alex is 2 years older than 6 times the age of Zander.
C) Alex is 4 years older than 3 times the age of Zander.
D) Alex is 2 years older than 3 times the age of Zander.
E) Alex is 1 year older than 6 times the age of Zander.

24) You need to fill a rectangular solid container with a liquid substance. The length of the rectangular solid is 12 feet, the width is 9 feet, and the volume is 1080 cubic feet. What is the height of the rectangular solid?
A) 10 feet
B) 12 feet
C) 90 feet
D) 100 feet
E) 120 feet

25) If $\frac{1}{5}x + 3 = 5$, then $x = ?$

A) $\frac{8}{5}$

B) $-\frac{8}{5}$

C) 8

D) 10

E) −10

26) The graph of a linear equation is shown below. Which one of the tables of values best represents the points on the graph?

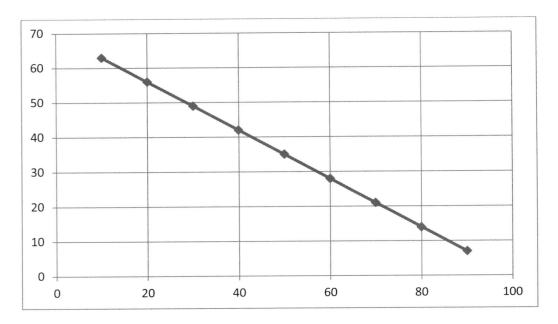

A)

x	y
5	65
10	64
15	63
20	62

B)

x	y
5	68
15	60
25	52
35	54

C)

x	y
10	63
20	56
30	49
40	42

D)

x	y
10	68
20	60
30	52
40	44

E)

x	y
30	42
40	35
50	28
60	21

27) An athlete ran 10 miles in 1.5 hours. The graph below shows the miles the athlete ran every 10 minutes. According to the graph, how many miles did the athlete run in the first 30 minutes?

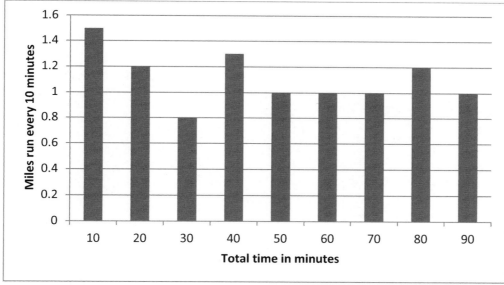

A) 0.8 miles
B) 2.0 miles
C) 3.0 miles
D) 3.4 miles
E) 3.5 miles

28) Which of the following steps will solve the equation for x: $18 = 3(x + 5)$
   A) Subtract 5 from each side of the equation, and then divide both sides by 3.
   B) Subtract 18 from each side of the equation, and then divide both sides by 5.
   C) Multiply both x and 5 by 3 on the right side of the equation. Then subtract 15 from each side of the equation.
   D) Divide each side of the equation by 3. Then subtract 5 from both sides of the equation.
   E) Divide each side of the equation by 5. Then subtract 3 from both sides of the equation.

29) A packaging company secures their packages with plastic strapping prior to shipment. The box is 18 inches in height, 16 inches in depth, and 38 inches in length. For certain packages, 14 extra inches of strapping is used to make a handle on the top of the package to carry it. The strapping is wrapped around the length and width of the entire package, as shown in the following diagram:

How many inches of strapping is needed to wrap 35 packages if no handles are used?
   A) 5,040
   B) 7,700
   C) 8,190
   D) 10,080
   E) 10,570

30) A clothing store sells jackets and jeans at a discount during a sales period. T represents the number of jackets sold and N represents the number of jeans sold. The total amount of money the store collected for sales of jeans and jackets during the sales period was $4,000. The amount of money earned from selling jackets was one-third of that earned from selling jeans. The jeans sold for $20 a pair. How many pairs of jeans did the store sell during the sales period?
   A)   15
   B)   20
   C)   150
   D)   200
   E) 3000

31) Mardetta is putting money into her checking account every week, and this weekly deposit is represented as x. After 40 weeks of putting money into her account, she took out or withdrew $180 from the account. The remaining balance on the account after the withdrawal was $1,020. Which equation below correctly expresses the balance of the account in D before the withdrawal and the 40 weekly deposits of x were made? Note that the account earns no interest.

A) $D = \$1{,}200 + 40x$
B) $D = \$1{,}080 + 40x$
C) $D - 40x = \$1{,}200$
D) $D + 40x = \$1{,}080$
E) $D = \$1{,}200 - 40x$

32) Which of the following is equivalent to the expression $36 - 2x$ for all values of x?

A) $6 + 2(15 - x)$
B) $6(6 - 2x)$
C) $39 - (3 - 2x)$
D) $8(5 - 2x) - 4$
E) $6(6 - 4x) - 2x$

33) Carlos is going to buy a house. The total purchase price of the house is represented by variable H. He will pay D dollars immediately, and then he will make equal payments (P) each month for M months. If H = $300,000, P = $700 and M = 360, how much will Carlos pay immediately?

A) $38,000
B) $48,000
C) $58,000
D) $252,000
E) $299,300

34) Which of the following equations is equivalent to $\frac{x}{5} \div \frac{9}{y}$?

A) $\frac{xy}{45}$

B) $\frac{9x}{5y}$

C) $\frac{1}{9} \times \frac{x}{5y}$

D) $\frac{1}{5} \times \frac{9}{5y}$

E) $\frac{1}{5} \div \frac{9x}{y}$

35) The radius (R) of circle A is 5 centimeters. The radius of circle B is 3 centimeters. Which of the following statements is true? You may select more than 1 answer.

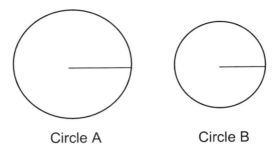

Circle A   Circle B

A) The difference between the areas of the circles is 2.
B) The difference between the areas of the circles is 9π.
C) The difference between the circumferences of the circles is 2.
D) The difference between the circumferences of the circles is 4π.
E) The difference between the diameters of the circles is 4.

36) Liz wants to put new vinyl flooring in her kitchen. She will buy the flooring in square pieces that measure 1 square foot each. The entire room is 8 feet by 12 feet. The cupboards are two feet deep from front to back. Flooring will not be put under the cupboards. A diagram of her kitchen is provided.

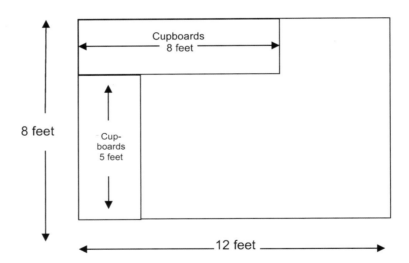

How many pieces of vinyl will Liz need to cover her floor?
A) 120
B) 96
C) 70
D) 84
E) 88

37) A large wheel (L) has a radius of 10 inches. A small wheel (S) has a radius of 6 inches. If the large wheel is going to travel 360 revolutions, how many more revolutions does the small wheel need to make to cover the same distance?
A) 120
B) 240
C) 360
D) 720
E) 120π

38) Look at the bar chart below and answer the question that follows.

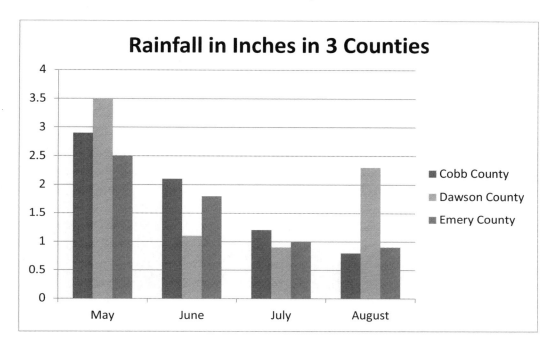

What was the approximate difference in the amount of rainfall for Dawson County and Emery County for June?
A) Dawson County had 0.6 more inches of rainfall than Emery County.
B) Emery County had 0.6 more inches of rainfall than Dawson County.
C) Dawson County had 1.1 fewer inches of rainfall than Emery County.
D) Emery County had 1.1 fewer inches of rainfall than Dawson County.
E) Emery County had 1.6 fewer inches of rainfall than Dawson County.

39) A farmer has a rectangular pen in which he keeps animals. He has decided to divide the pen into two parts. To divide the pen, he will erect a fence diagonally from the two corners, as shown in the diagram below. How long in yards is the diagonal fence?

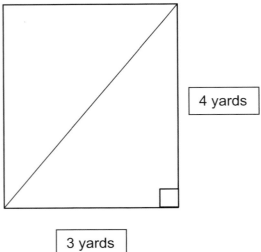

4 yards

3 yards

A) 4
B) 5
C) 5.5
D) 6
E) 6.5

40) The diagram below shows a figure made from a semicircle, a rectangle, and an equilateral triangle. The rectangle has a length of 18 inches and a width of 10 inches. What is the perimeter of the figure?

A) 56 inches + 5π inches
B) 56 inches + 10π inches
C) 56 inches + 12.5π inches
D) 56 inches + 25π inches
E) 208.9 inches + 12.5π inches

41)	Read the problem below and then answer the question that follows.

> • Paul leaves his house at 5:30 to go running.
> • He runs 2 miles north through town, then continues 3 miles further north past town.
> • He then runs south to his house along the same route.
> • What is Paul's running pace?

What piece of information is needed in order to answer the problem?
A) The number of steps that Paul makes.
B) The time that Paul returns home.
C) The length of Paul's stride.
D) The length of the return journey.
E) No further information is required.

42)	Look at the table below and answer the question that follows.

Disease or Complication	Percentage of patients with this disease that have survived and total number of patients
Cardiopulmonary and vascular	82% (602,000)
HIV/AIDS	73% (215,000)
Diabetes	89% (793,000)
Cancer and leukemia	48% (231,000)
Premature birth complications	64% (68,000)

The total number of deaths from the two least fatal diseases amounted to which figure below?
A) 82,530
B) 208,960
C) 1,186,040
D) 1,199,410
E) 1,919,410

43) The illustration below shows a pentagon. The shaded part at the top of the pentagon has a height of 6 inches.

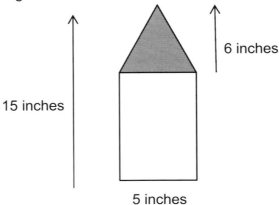

15 inches

6 inches

5 inches

The height of the entire pentagon is 15 inches, and the base of the pentagon is 5 inches. What fraction expresses the area of the shaded part to the area of the entire pentagon? State your answer as a simplified fraction in the spaces provided.

Numerator value = _____

Denominator value = _____

Go on to the next page.

44)   Look at the graph below and answer the question that follows.

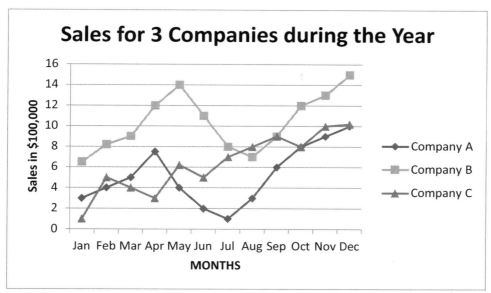

The combined total of sales for all three of the companies was greatest during which month of the year?

A) December
B) November
C) May
D) April
E) January

45)   In the figure below, *x* and *y* are parallel lines, and line *z* is a transversal crossing both *x* and *y*. Which three angles are equal in measure? You may select more than one answer.

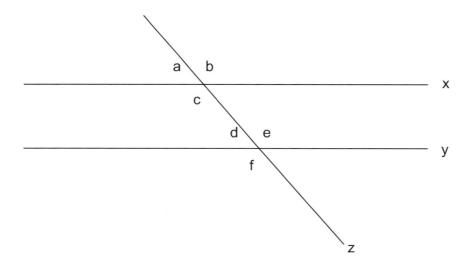

A) ∠a, ∠b, ∠c
B) ∠b, ∠c, ∠f
C) ∠b, ∠e, ∠f
D) ∠a, ∠d, ∠e
E) ∠a, ∠d, ∠f

46) What is the median of the numbers in the following list:
2.5, 9.4, 3.1, 1.7, 3.2, 8.2, 4.5, 6.4, 7.8
A) 3.2
B) 4.5
C) 5.2
D) 6.4
E) 7.7

47) Suki rolls a fair pair of six-sided dice. Each die has values from 1 to 6. She rolls an even number on her first roll. What is the probability that she will roll an odd number on her next roll?
A) $1/2$
B) $1/6$
C) $2/6$
D) $6/11$
E) $5/11$

48) The state highway department wants to find out how the residents of Buford feel about a new road being constructed around their town. Which one of the following methods will result in the most statistically valid information about the opinions of the residents at the town?
A) To question drivers of a random selection of vehicles traveling through Buford
B) To poll drivers at random as they exit the interstate highway near Buford
C) To ask car owners living in Buford to participate in a survey
D) To select a random sample of names from Buford's voting register
E) To select participants for a survey from a list of all of the citizens living in Buford

49) A student receives the following scores on his exams during the semester:
89, 65, 75, 68, 82, 74, 86
What is the mean of his scores?
A) 24
B) 74
C) 75
D) 77
E) 82

50) A clown pulls balloons out of a bag at random to blow up and give to children during a birthday party. At the start of the party, there are 10 red balloons, 7 green balloons, 6 purple balloons, 5 orange balloons, and 11 blue balloons in the bag. The clown selects the first balloon, which is blue, and gives it to the first child. If the second child gets an orange balloon, what is the probability that the third child will get a blue balloon?

A) $^{11}/_{37}$

B) $^{10}/_{37}$

C) $^{11}/_{39}$

D) $^{10}/_{39}$

E) $^{1}/_{11}$

51) What is the mode of the numbers in the following list:
1.6, 2.9, 4.5, 2.5, 2.6, 5.1, 5.4
A) 3.5
B) 3.1
C) 3.0
D) 2.5
E) no mode

52) Sam was adding up the following numbers. However, when he put the numbers into the calculator, he accidently swapped the digits on one of the numbers. His erroneous sum is off by 36. Which number did he enter incorrectly into his calculator?
59
82
14
35
+ 97

A) 14
B) 35
C) 59
D) 82
E) 97

53) There are 10 cars in a parking lot. Nine of the cars are 2, 3, 4, 5, 6, 7, 9, 10, and 12 years old, respectively. If the average age of the 10 cars is 6 years old, how old is the 10th car?
A) 1 year old
B) 2 years old
C) 3 years old
D) 4 years old
E) 5 years old

54) Which of the following are statistical questions? You may select more than one answer.

_____ (1) What size shoe does Mrs. Shapiro wear?

_____ (2) How many residents of the town oppose the tax increase?

_____ (3) Will it rain tomorrow?

_____ (4) How many miles can that car travel on a tank of gasoline?

_____ (5) Do most college graduates in our state find jobs within one year of

leaving college?

55) The range and mean of 5 numbers are 10 and 14 respectively. The five numbers are positive integers greater than 0. If the range is increased by 2, which of the following could be true of the numbers in the new set? You may select more than one answer.
A) The highest number is increased by 2.
B) The highest number is increased by 1 and the lowest number is decreased by 1.
C) The highest number is decreased by 1 and the lowest number is increased by 1.
D) The lowest number is increased by 2.
E) The mean of the numbers remains unchanged

56) A deck of cards contains 13 hearts, 13 diamonds, 13 clubs, and 13 spades. Cards are selected from the deck at random. Once selected, the cards are discarded and are not placed back into the deck. Two spades, one heart, and a club are drawn from the deck. What is the probability that the next card drawn from the deck will be a heart?

A) $1/13$

B) $1/12$

C) $13/52$

D) $13/48$

E) $1/4$

Praxis Core Math Practice Set 3 – Answer Key

1) D

2) D

3) C

4) E

5) C

6) C

7) E

8) A

9) B

10) B

11) C

12) B

13) C

14) A

15) B

16) C

17) C

18) C

19) C

20) A

21) E

22) A

23) B

24) A

25) D

26) C

27) E

28) D

29) B

30) C

31) E

32) A

33) B

34) A

35) D and E

36) C

37) B

38) B

39) B

40) A

41) B

42) A

43) numerator value = 1; denominator value = 4

44) A

45) B and C

46) B

47) A

48) E

49) D

50) B

51) E

52) C

53) B

54) 2 and 5

55) A and B

56) E

Praxis Core Math Practice Set 3 – Solutions and Explanations

1) The correct answer is D. Remember to look at the first item in the expression, as well as the numerator of the final item in the expression in order to understand the conversion:

   10 **kilometers** × 1000 meters/1 kilometer × 100 **centimeters**/1 meter

   In other words, she is converting kilometers to centimeters.

2) The correct answer is D. We have the following numbers in our problem:

   0.0012
   0.0253
   0.2135
   0.3152

   If you still do not feel confident with decimals, remember that you can remove the decimal point and the zeroes after the decimal but before the other integers in order to see the answer more clearly.

   12
   253
   2135
   3152

3) The correct answer is C. If $\frac{x}{24}$ is between 8 and 9, x will need to be between 192 and 216, since $\frac{192}{24}$ =192 ÷ 24 = 8 and $\frac{216}{24}$ = 216 ÷ 24 = 9. 200 is the only number from the answer choices that is greater than 192 and less than 216.

4) The correct answer is E. The ratio of bags of apples to bags of oranges is 2 to 3, so for every two bags of apples, there are three bags of oranges. First, take the total amount of bags of apples and divide by 2: 44 ÷ 2 = 22. Then multiply this by 3 to determine how many bags of oranges are in the store: 22 × 3 = 66

5) The correct answer is C. If Ali uses a jar of coffee every week, he needs 52 jars to last a year since there are 52 weeks in a year.

6) The correct answer is C. Work backwards based on the facts given. There are 18 students left at the end after one-fourth of them left for the principal's office. So, set up an equation for this:

$18 + ^1/_4T = T$

$18 + ^1/_4T - ^1/_4T = T - ^1/_4T$

$18 = ^3/_4T$

$18 \times 4 = ^3/_4T \times 4$

$72 = 3T$

$72 \div 3 = 3T \div 3$

$24 = T$

So, before the group of pupils left to see the principal, there were 24 students in the class. We know that one-fifth of the students left at the beginning to go to singing lessons, so we need to set up an equation for this:

$24 + ^1/_5T = T$

$24 + ^1/_5T - ^1/_5T = T - ^1/_5T$

$24 = ^4/_5T$

$24 \times 5 = ^4/_5T \times 5$

$120 = 4T$

$120 \div 4 = 4T \div 4$

$30 = T$

7) The correct answer is E. He needs to subtract the 92 that he added by mistake to get back to his starting point. Then he needs to subtract 92 again to get the correct result. So, he can subtract 92 two times or simply shortcut by subtracting 184.

8) The correct answer is A. Chantelle correctly answered 12 out of 15 questions, so she incorrectly answered 3 questions (15 − 12 = 3). This can be expressed as the fraction 3/15, which can be simplified to 1/5.

9) The correct answer is B. At the beginning of January, there are 300 students, but 5% of the students leave during the month, so we have 95% left at the end of the month: 300 × 95% = 285. Then 15 students join on the last day of the month, so we

add that back in to get to the total at the end of January: 285 + 15 = 300. If this pattern continues, there will always be 300 students in the academy at the end of any month.

10) The correct answer is B. The question is asking us to calculate one third of one half. So, we multiply to get our answer: $\frac{1}{2} \times \frac{1}{3} = \frac{(1 \times 1)}{(2 \times 3)} = \frac{1}{6}$. This is represented by the dark gray area in graph B.

11) The correct answer is C. The question is asking us how many residents have more than 3 relatives nearby, so we need to add the bars for 4 and 5 relatives from the chart. 20 residents have 4 relatives nearby and 10 residents have 5 relatives nearby, so 30 residents (20 + 10 = 30) have more than 3 relatives nearby.

12) The correct answer is B. In an isosceles tringle, two angles will have equal measurements. These two angles are known as congruent angles. In other words, congruent means equal in measurement. So, first of all, add the two congruent angles together: 49 + 49 = 98. Remember that the sum of all of the angles in a triangle must be equal to 180 degrees. So, subtract the sum of the congruent angles from 180 to solve: 180 − 98 = 82

13) The correct answer is C. Divide by the fractional hour in order to determine the speed for an entire hour: 38.4 miles ÷ $\frac{4}{5}$ of an hour = 38.4 × $\frac{5}{4}$ = (38 × 5) ÷ 4 = 48 mph

14) The correct answer is A. The ratio of defective chips to functioning chips is 1 to 20. So, the defective chips form one group and the functioning chips form another group. Therefore, the total data set can be divided into groups of 21. Accordingly, $\frac{1}{21}$ of the chips will be defective. The factory produced 11,235 chips last week, so we calculate as follows: 11,235 × $\frac{1}{21}$ = 535

15) The correct answer is B. The total amount available is $55,000, so we can substitute this for C in the equation provided in order to calculate R number of residents:

C = $750R + $2,550

$55,000 = $750R + $2,550

$55,000 − $2,550 = $750R + $2,550 − $2,550

$55,000 − $2,550 = $750R

$52,450 = \$750R$

$52,450 \div \$750 = \$750R \div \$750$

$52,450 \div \$750 = R$

$69.9 = R$

It is not possible to accommodate a fractional part of one person, so we need to round down to 69 residents.

16) The correct answer is C. The value of μ must be greater than $^{11}/_3$, which is equal to 3.6667. The answer 4.1 is the only option which meets this criterion.

17) The correct answer is C. There are 2 stars for speeding, and each star equals 30 violations, so there were 60 speeding violations in total. The fine for speeding is $50 per violation, so the total amount collected for speeding violations was: 60 speeding violations × $50 per violation = $3000. There are three stars for other violations, which is equal to 90 violations (3 × 30 = 90). Other violations are $20 each, so the total for other violations is: 90 × $20 = $1800. Next, we need to deduct these two amounts from the total collections of $6,000 in order to find out how much was collected for parking violations: $6000 − $3000 − $1800 = $1200 in total for parking violations. There is one star for parking violations, so there were 30 parking violations. We divide to get the answer: $1200 income for parking violations ÷ 30 parking violations = $40 each

18) The correct answer is C. We know that at 10:30 he is 210 miles from Georgetown. If he is traveling 70 miles per hour, he would need 3 more hours to get to Georgetown since 3 × 70 = 210. So, he would arrive at 1:30 if he had not taken a break. But we need to add in a 30-minute break, so he will arrive in Georgetown at 2:00 pm.

19) The correct answer is C. Take the total dollar amount of the budget and multiply by the 21% for public safety: $6,537,200 × 0.21 = $1,372,812

20) The correct answer is A. We cannot calculate the number of students in the class with belts of particular colors because we do not know the color of the belts the new students. The problem is telling us how many students there are in each group and how many of each group have left. The problem also tells us how many students in total have joined, so we can calculate the new total number of students.

21) The correct answer is E. The original price of the sofa on Wednesday was x. On Thursday, the sofa was reduced by 10%, so the price on Thursday was 90% of x or $0.90x$. On Friday, the sofa was reduced by a further 15%, so the price on Friday was 85% of the price on Thursday, so we can multiply Thursday's price by 0.85 to get our answer: $(0.90)(0.85)x$

22) The correct answer is A. First, calculate the total area represented on the diagram: 9 × 7 = 63 square yards in total. Then count the gray squares for the reservoir. We can see that there are 18 gray squares. So, we know that the gray area is 18 square yards and the white area is 45 square yards, since 63 − 18 = 45. So, the ratio is 18:45. Both of these numbers are divisible by 9, so we can simplify the ratio to 2:5 because 18 ÷ 9 = 2 and 45 ÷ 9 = 5.

23) The correct answer is B. Assign a variable for the age of each boy. Alex = A, Burt = B, and Zander = Z. Alex is twice as old as Burt, so A = 2B. Burt is one year older than three times the age of Zander, so B = 3Z + 1. Then substitute the value of B into the first equation.

A = 2B

A = 2(3Z + 1)

A = 6Z + 2

So, Alex is 2 years older than 6 times the age of Zander.

24) The correct answer is A. From the formula sheet, we know that the formula for the volume of a rectangular is: solid = length × width × height. Here, we are given the volume (the larger number of 1080), so we need to divide that by the length and then the width in order to find the height: (1080 ÷ 12) ÷ 9 = 90 ÷ 9 = 10 feet

25) The correct answer is D. Get the integers to one side of the equation first of all.

$$\frac{1}{5}x + 3 = 5$$

$$\frac{1}{5}x + 3 - 3 = 5 - 3$$

$$\frac{1}{5}x = 2$$

Then multiply to eliminate the fraction and solve the problem.

$$\frac{1}{5}x \times 5 = 2 \times 5$$

$$x = 10$$

26) The correct answer is C. The first point on the graph lies at $x = 10$, so we can eliminate answer choices A and B. The point for the y coordinate that corresponds to $x = 10$ is 63 not 68, so we can eliminate answer choice D. The point for the y coordinate that corresponds to $x = 30$ is 49 not 42, so we can also eliminate answer choice E.

27) The correct answer is E. The first three bars of the graph represent the first 30 minutes, so add these three amounts together for your answer: 1.5 + 1.2 + 0.8 = 3.5 miles

28) The correct answer is D. Divide each side of the equation by 3. Then subtract 5 from both sides of the equation as shown below.

$$18 = 3(x + 5)$$

$$18 \div 3 = [3(x + 5)] \div 3$$

$$6 = x + 5$$

$$6 - 5 = x + 5 - 5$$

$$1 = x$$

29) The correct answer is B. Calculate the length of strapping for the piece that goes over the front of the package: 38 + 16 + 38 + 16 = 108. Then calculate the length of strapping for the piece that goes over the top of the package: 38 + 18 + 38 + 18 = 112. Without the handle, we need 108 + 112 = 220 inches per package. 220 inches per package × 35 packages = 7,700 total inches

30) The correct answer is C. If the amount earned from selling jackets was one-third that of selling jeans, the ratio of jacket to jean sales was 1 to 3. So, we need to divide the total sales of $4,000 into $1,000 for jackets and $3,000 for jeans. We can then solve as follows: $3,000 in jeans sales ÷ $20 per pair = 150 pairs sold

31) The correct answer is E. We are being asked for the balance of the account before the withdrawal and the 40 weekly deposits. There was $1,020 in the account after the $180 withdrawal, so add the withdrawal back in to get the balance at that point in time: $1,020 + $80 = $1,200. Then subtract the amount of the deposits to get the balance at the start: $1,200 − 40$x$. So, E is the correct answer.

32) The correct answer is A. For algebraic equivalency questions like this, you can perform the operations on each of the answer choices to see which one is equivalent. Remember to be careful when performing multiplication on negative numbers inside parentheticals.

$6 + 2(15 - x) =$

$6 + (2 \times 15) + (2 \times -x) =$

$6 + 30 - 2x =$

$36 - 2x$

33) The correct answer is B. The total of the monthly payments is:

$700 per month × 360 months = $252,000

The total price of the house is $300,000 so deduct the total payments from this amount in order to calculate the immediate payment: $300,000 − $252,000 = $48,000

34) The correct answer is A. To divide, invert the second fraction and then multiply as shown.

$$\frac{x}{5} \div \frac{9}{y} = \frac{x}{5} \times \frac{y}{9} = \frac{x \times y}{5 \times 9} = \frac{xy}{45}$$

35) The correct answers are D and E. The formula for the area of a circle is: πR^2. The area of circle A is $\pi \times 5^2 = 25\pi$ and the area of circle B is $\pi \times 3^2 = 9\pi$. So, the difference between the areas is 16π.

The formula for circumference is: $\pi 2R$. The circumference of circle A is $\pi \times 2 \times 5 = 10\pi$ and the circumference for circle B is $\pi \times 2 \times 3 = 6\pi$. The difference in the circumferences is 4π. So, answer D is correct.

Diameter is equal to the radius times 2, so the diameter of circle A is 10 and the diameter of circle B is 6, and the difference in diameters is 4. So, answer E is also correct.

36) The correct answer is C. Calculate the area for each of the cupboards: 8 × 2 = 16 and 5 × 2 = 10. Therefore, the total area for both cupboards is 16 + 10 = 26. Then find the area for the entire kitchen: 8 × 12 = 96. Then deduct the cupboards from the total: 96 − 26 = 70

37) The correct answer is B. Circumference is $2\pi R$, so the circumference of the large wheel is 20π and the circumference of the smaller wheel is 12π. If the large wheel travels 360 revolutions, it travels a distance of: $20\pi \times 360 = 7200\pi$. To determine the number of revolutions the small wheel needs to make to go the same distance, we divide the distance by the circumference of the smaller wheel: $7200\pi \div 12\pi = 600$. Finally, calculate the difference in the number of revolutions: $600 − 360 = 240$

38) The correct answer is B. In June, Dawson County had 1.1 inches of rain and Emery County had 1.7 inches. Therefore, Emery County had 0.6 more inches of rainfall than Dawson County.

39) The correct answer is B. The two sides of the field form a right angle, so we can use the Pythagorean theorem to find the length of the hypotenuse to solve the problem: $\sqrt{3^2 + 4^2} = \sqrt{9 + 16} = \sqrt{25} = 5$

40) The correct answer is A. First, we need to find the circumference of the semicircle on the left side of the figure. The width of the rectangle of 10 inches forms the diameter of the semicircle, so the circumference of an entire circle with a diameter of 10 inches would be 10π inches. We need the circumference for a semicircle only, which is half of a circle, so we need to divide the circumference by 2: $10\pi \div 2 = 5\pi$. Since the right side of the figure is an equilateral triangle, the two sides of the triangle have the same length as the width of the rectangle, so they are 10 inches each. Finally, you need to add up the lengths of all of the sides to get the answer: 18 + 18 + 10 + 10 + 5π = 56 + 5π inches

41) The correct answer is B. We know that Paul will have run ten miles when he finishes since he runs 5 miles north, then returns and goes 5 miles south. The question is asking about his running pace or speed. In order to know speed, we need to know the distance traveled and the amount of time it takes to travel the distance. So, we

know the distance, but not the time. Accordingly, we would need to know what time he gets back home in order to solve the problem.

42) The correct answer is A. You need to determine the death rate, so subtract the survival rate from 100% to get the death rate for each category. Then multiply for each category and compare:

Cardiopulmonary and vascular deaths: 602,000 × 0.18 = 108,360

HIV/AIDS deaths: 215,000 × 0.27 = 58,050

Diabetes deaths: 793,000 × 0.11 = 87,230

Cancer and leukemia deaths: 231,000 × 0.52 =120,120

Deaths from premature birth complications: 68,000 × 0.36 = 24,480

Then add the two smallest amounts together to solve: 24,480 + 58,050 = 82,530

43) The correct answer is a numerator value of 1 and a denominator value of 4. Calculate the area of the triangle: $\frac{1}{2} \times base \times height = \frac{1}{2} \times 5 \times 6 = \frac{1}{2} \times 30 = 15$. The height of the unshaded part is 9 inches since $15 - 6 = 9$, so next we can calculate the area of the unshaded rectangular part: $base \times height = 5 \times 9 = 45$. Add the area of the unshaded part of the figure to the area of the triangle in order to get the area for the entire figure: $45 + 15 = 60$. Finally, express the result as a simplified fraction with the area of the triangle in the numerator and the area of the entire figure in the denominator: $^{15}/_{60} = ^{1}/_{4}$

44) The correct answer is A. We can see that December has the highest figure for all three of the lines. Accordingly, December will also have the greatest combined sales for all three companies.

45) The correct answers are B and C. When a transversal crosses two parallel lines, opposite angles will be equal in measure and corresponding angles will also be equal in measure. (Corresponding angles are angles in the matching same-shaped corners.) Angles $\angle b$ and $\angle c$ are opposite angles and angles $\angle c$ and $\angle f$ are corresponding angles, so answer B is correct. Angles $\angle b$ and $\angle e$ are corresponding and angles $\angle e$ and $\angle f$ are opposite, so answer C is also correct.

46) The correct answer is B. Our data set is: 2.5, 9.4, 3.1, 1.7, 3.2, 8.2, 4.5, 6.4, 7.8. First, put the numbers in ascending order: 1.7, 2.5, 3.1, 3.2, 4.5, 6.4, 7.8, 8.2, 9.4. The median is the number in the middle of the set: 1.7, 2.5, 3.1, 3.2, **4.5**, 6.4, 7.8, 8.2, 9.4

47) The correct answer is A. The outcome of an earlier roll does not affect the outcome of the next roll. When rolling a pair of dice, the possibility of an odd number is always $1/2$, just as the possibility of an even number is always $1/2$. We can prove this mathematically by looking at the possible outcomes:

1,1 1,2 1,3 1,4 1,5 1,6

2,1 2,2 2,3 2,4 2,5 2,6

3,1 3,2 3,3 3,4 3,5 3,6

4,1 4,2 4,3 4,4 4,5 4,6

5,1 5,2 5,3 5,4 5,5 5,6

6,1 6,2 6,3 6,4 6,5 6,6

The odd number combinations are highlighted:

1,1 **1,2** 1,3 **1,4** 1,5 **1,6**

2,1 2,2 **2,3** 2,4 **2,5** 2,6

3,1 **3,2** 3,3 **3,4** 3,5 **3,6**

4,1 4,2 **4,3** 4,4 **4,5** 4,6

5,1 **5,2** 5,3 **5,4** 5,5 **5,6**

6,1 6,2 **6,3** 6,4 **6,5** 6,6

So, we can see that an odd number will be rolled half of the time.

48) The correct answer is E. The proposed course of action affects the residents of Buford, so the statistical sample must represent these residents as much as possible. The most representative sample would therefore be achieved by selecting participants for a survey from a list of all of the citizens living in Buford. Answers A

and B may represent people living in other areas who are merely driving near Buford. Answers C and D would fail to represent residents of Buford who do not drive or who have not registered to vote.

49) The correct answer is D. To find the mean, add up all of the items in the set and then divide by the number of items in the set. Here we have 7 numbers in the set, so we get our answer as follows: (89 + 65 + 75 + 68 + 82 + 74 + 86) ÷ 7 = 539 ÷ 7 = 77

50) The correct answer is B. At the start of the party, there are 10 red balloons, 7 green balloons, 6 purple balloons, 5 orange balloons, and 11 blue balloons in the bag, so we add all of these up to get our data set at the beginning: 10 + 7 + 6 + 5 + 11 = 39 items in the data set at the beginning. Then a blue balloon and an orange balloon are removed, so we need to reduce the data set for these two items: 39 − 2 = 37. The problem is asking about the probability of a blue balloon. There are 11 blue balloons at the start and one has been removed, so there are 10 blue balloons left. Remember to express the probability as a fraction with the possibility of the outcome in the numerator and the remaining data set in the denominator: $^{10}/_{37}$

51) The correct answer is E. We have the data set: 1.6, 2.9, 4.5, 2.5, 2.6, 5.1, 5.4 The mode is the number that occurs most frequently. All of the numbers only occur once. So, there is no mode.

52) The correct answer is C. Swap the digits on each of the numbers and subtract to find the one that is off by 36. In doing so, we discover that Sam entered 95 when he should have entered 59, because the difference is 36: 95 − 59 = 36.

53) The correct answer is B. We don't know the age of the 10th car, so put this in as x to solve: (2 + 3 + 4 + 5 + 6 + 7 + 9 + 10 + 12 + x) ÷ 10 = 6

[(2 + 3 + 4 + 5 + 6 + 7 + 9 + 10 + 12 + x) ÷ 10] × 10 = 6 × 10

2 + 3 + 4 + 5 + 6 + 7 + 9 + 10 + 12 + x = 60

58 + x = 60

x = 2

54) The correct answers are (2) and (5). Statistical questions ask about behaviors or opinions. So, the following are statistical questions: "How many residents of the

town oppose the tax increase?" and "Do most college graduates in our state find jobs within one year of leaving college?"

55) The correct answers are A and B. The range is the difference between the highest number and the lowest number in a data set. If the range increases by 2, then the highest number could go up by 2 or the highest and lowest numbers could increase and decrease by 1 each respectively.

56) The correct answer is E. We have 54 cards in the deck (13 × 4 = 52). We have taken out two spades, one heart, and a club, thereby removing 4 cards. So, the available data set is 48 (52 − 4 = 48). The desired outcome is drawing a heart. We have 13 hearts to begin with and one has been removed, so there are 12 hearts left. So, the probability of drawing a heart is $^{12}/_{48} = ^{1}/_{4}$

Appendix – Formula Sheet

Distance:
1 foot = 12 inches
1 yard = 3 feet
1 meter = 1,000 millimeters
1 meter = 100 centimeters

Rectangle and box perimeter:
perimeter = 2(*length* + *width*)

Area of squares and rectangles:
area = *length* × *width*

Volume of rectangular or square solid:
Length × Width × Height

Circles:
number of degrees in circle = 360°
circumference = π × *diameter*
area = π × (*radius*)^2
$\pi \approx 3.14$

Triangles:
sum of angles = 180°
area = ½ (*base* × *height*)
hypotenuse length: $\sqrt{A^2 + B^2} = C$
The hypotenuse is the diagonal side of a triangle, opposite the right angle.

Straight Lines:
sum of two supplementary angles = 180°
Note that supplementary angles are side-by-side on a straight line.

Made in the USA
Middletown, DE
15 October 2021

50398953R00073